From Voodoo to Viagra
The Magic of Medicine

From Voodoo to Viagra

The Magic of Medicine

37 Uplifting Essays from a Doctor's Bag of Tricks

Oscar London, M.D., W.B.D.

author of *Kill as Few Patients as Possible*

Ten Speed Press

Berkeley / Toronto

★

TO

My Mother Lil

1905–2000

Ten Speed Press
Box 7123
Berkeley, California 94707
www.tenspeed.com

★

Distributed in Australia by Simon & Schuster Australia, in Canada by Ten Speed Press Canada, in New Zealand by Southern Publishers Group, in South Africa by Real Books, in Southeast Asia by Berkeley Books, and in the United Kingdom and Europe by Airlift Book Company.

Some of these essays were originally published on the medical Web site, HealthCentral.com

Cover and text design by Jeff Puda

Library of Congress Cataloging-in-Publication Data
London, Oscar.
     From voodoo to viagra, the magic of medicine : 37 uplifting essays from a doctor's bag of tricks / by Oscar London.
         p. cm.
     ISBN 1-58008-287-4
     1. Medicine–Humor. 2. Medicine–Anecdotes. I. Title.

★

R705 .L66 2001
610–dc21

                                                                2001017417

Printed in Canada
First printing, 2001

1 2 3 4 5 6 7 8 9 10 — 05 04 03 02 01

Contents

1

Mouth Wide Shut

Oh, if only Stanley Kubrick had lived to direct my life in medicine!

His last film, *Eyes Wide Shut*, tells the story of Dr. William Harford (Tom Cruise), a young, handsome Manhattan internist who works in what appears to be a five-thousand-dollar long white coat by Brioni. His practice consists of seeing four patients a day in a spacious office with eight assistants, knee-deep rugs, and black marble countertops.

He is married to Alice (Nicole Kidman), an incandescent beauty and art curator, who spends more than half her life naked. They live with Helena, their fashionably only child, age seven, in an unspeakably swank Upper East Side townhouse.

After a less than exhausting day in the office, Dr. Harford and his wife attend a party thrown by Victor Ziegler (Sidney Pollack), one of his billionaire patients, in a mansion that makes Versailles look like a Motel 6.

By subtle contrast, I'm a Berkeley internist with a practice that requires me to see twenty-five HMO patients a day in a small, fifty-year-old office that was recently given six months to live by a specialist in dry rot. My yearly income is considerably less than Dr. Harford's monthly office rent.

Of course it's not fair to compare my marriage to that portrayed by Tom Cruise and Nicole Kidman, since my wife and I are more of the Vivien Leigh-Clark Gable type couple. As befitting our lower socio-economic class, we have twice as many children as the Harfords.

Our son and daughter, now grown, had to suffer toys purchased from K-Mart and upscale garage sales as opposed to Helena Harford, who has a charge account and personal shopper at FAO Schwarz. As a result of seeing this movie, our kids never call us.

Last year, while Kubrick was directing the billionaire's caviar and champagne party, my wife and I attended a potluck fund-raiser for the Berkeley Needle Exchange Program. It was held in the Mimi Epstein-Gomez Room of the local Center for Homeless Parents of Gays and Lesbians. (A fund-raiser to renovate the Mimi Epstein-Gomez Room was taking place in the basement.) As opposed to the live dance orchestra the size of the New York Philharmonic in the movie, we were afflicted with an over-amped CD of the Grateful Dead.

During his night at the lavish party, Dr. Harford is called upstairs to the host's ornate bedroom where he's asked to minister to a gorgeous, naked prostitute who had suddenly become comatose after making love to Victor Ziegler (Sidney Pollack).

To this medical viewer, the differential diagnosis was heroin overdose versus near-terminal boredom from having spent the better part of an evening submitting to Sidney Pollack.

With consummate skill, Dr. Harford jiggles the head of the call girl a bit, says a few encouraging words and, lo!, she revives. Not wearing any clothes, the woman is unable to produce her Blue Cross card, but Pollack indicates to Cruise that he'll take care of it, and then some.

At the potluck—as opposed to the Pollack—affair, I must have seen twenty people just as stoned as the prostitute in the movie. But they remained fully clothed, semiupright, and somewhat less than gorgeous. After we were introduced, one of them asked me if I carried any morphine in my doctor's bag.

The next evening Dr. Harford, to my astonishment, responds to another house call. When he arrives, the patient, billionaire number two, is comfortably dead and neatly tucked into his king-sized bed. There's not much for Dr. Harford to do but check the patient's eyeballs and console the deceased's beautiful blonde daughter. He has not said three words before the daughter throws herself at him, kisses him with maximum passion, and professes her love for him.

Many years ago I made a house call. I don't remember exactly when or precisely why. But I do recall that the elderly patient's son, a haggard, unshaven man in his fifties, threw a copy of the *Columbia Desk Encyclopedia* at me (and missed) when I refused to hospitalize his father.

Spurning the grieving daughter's advances, Dr. Harford phones his partially undressed wife. He informs her that he'll be "detained" at the house call (something about waiting for out-of-town relatives to arrive).

After extricating himself from the love-smitten heiress, Dr. Harford impulsively follows a comely prostitute (number two) into her apartment where, after an agony of indecision, he pays her the going rate of $150 without laying a hand on her.

I'm reminded of one day in my office, during the era of fee-for-service medicine, when a beautiful, young female patient saw me at length for an initial visit. She finally decided that I wasn't her kind of physician and left my office, refusing to pay my $150 fee. Stanley Kubrick would *never* have let her get away with that.

Meanwhile, back on the set: Still seething over a remark his wife had made about her sexual fantasy involving a naval officer, Dr. Harford rents a costume at midnight and takes a cab to yet another (and grander) mansion. Uttering the stolen password, "Fidelio," he proceeds to crash an orgy.

Wearing a mask and cape, he walks and gawks through the mansion, while all about him are being committed random acts of fornication and senseless acts of cinematography. The masked participants are made up of old farts and young tarts.

Somehow, he doesn't fit in.

In a strange way this scene reminds me of the first time I walked into an operating room during my internship. Wearing a mask and gown, I was ordered by the elderly surgeon to stand next to his shapely scrub nurse. Kubrick's lens would have zoomed in on the fear and helplessness in my eyes.

Dazzled by the bright overhead lights and numbed by the frigid temperature of the OR, I stood mute while all about me were being committed gory acts of evisceration and bloody acts of hemostasis. Somehow, I didn't fit in.

So I became an internist.

2

Krispy Kremes: New Arthritis Wonder Drug?

FOR THE PAST TWO YEARS I'VE BEEN OBSESSED with the desire to taste a Krispy Kreme doughnut. In Berkeley, the Foodie Capital of the West, the word-of-mouth hype for this fabled confection has been so compelling that in recent months I've had to give myself atropine injections lest I drool in front of my patients.

Last March a chubby urologist of my acquaintance bolted his practice and his family to join a band of cultists waiting in line at the nearest Krispy Kreme shrine in Las Vegas. His wife hired two private eyes and a cult-debriefing therapist to retrieve him, and wouldn't you know it? At the first whiff of Krispy Kreme vapors emanating from the chimney of the shrine, the private eyes and therapist took their own places in line.

And then last month my prayers were almost answered when a Krispy Kreme franchise opened in Union City, California, just thirty miles from Berkeley. I vowed to make a pilgrimage to Union City the following weekend, but newspaper accounts began describing mob violence and near-riots among wannabe customers stuck in endless lines. At one point the sugar-starved protesters allegedly had to be hosed down with warm 7-Up.

One of my elderly patients was brought in by his family for exhaustion and uncontrollable shaking after actually ordering two dozen Krispy Kremes in Union City. He refused to disclose to his distraught family where he had been for the previous thirty-six hours, but an astute daughter-in-law detected a faint rime of sugar glaze above his upper lip. He broke down and confessed.

When the family dragged him into my office, I shared his loved ones' fury at his not bringing back any Krispy Kremes to Berkeley. "I couldn't stop!" he sobbed. "I ate them in the car! Threw the carton out the window! Damn cop cited me for littering when I told him I'd eaten the last one! Oh God!"

"There, there, Walt," I said through clenched, wet teeth. I sent him to the ER for an IV infusion of glucose in water to treat his profound hypoglycemia, a common occurrence many hours after an overdose of carbohydrates. He recovered promptly, but it's safe to say he suffered extreme elder abuse at the hands of his family on the drive back to their home.

Last Monday a highly ambitious drug rep, whom I'll call Hank, paid me one of his routine, thrice-weekly visits. For months he'd been trying to convince me to prescribe his company's stomach-friendly antiarthritis drug rather than its detested rival, an equally effective medication. He always brought three large cups of Starbuck's lattes and dozens of almond biscotti for my secretary, my bookkeeper, and me. He had treated my wife and me to blowouts at six of the finest Bay Area restaurants because, as he put it, he "liked" us.

Perversely I persisted in prescribing the rival drug because, as I put it, I "liked" it. Last Monday I ushered him into the sanctum sanctorum of my back consultation room, closed the door, and told him, "Hank, if you bring in a dozen warm Krispy Kremes from Union City by tomorrow, I'll prescribe your drug not only to every one of my arthritic patients but to the next hundred people who walk through that door—no matter what's wrong with them!"

The operative word in my request was "warm," because if there is one element essential to experiencing Krispy Kreme rapture it is heat, the feverish agitation of sugar and grease molecules that set in motion a chain reaction in the taste buds culminating in Nirvana, that is, disinterested wisdom and compassion, except for the desire to kill for a cup of coffee.

If you possibly detect in my offer to Hank a momentary lapse of medical ethics, let me assure you that Hank's drug has practically no side effects and, more likely than not, the next hundred people to walk through my door will have arthritic symptoms out the wazoo, so to speak. Well, frankly, under the circumstances, I don't care WHAT you think.

A little after 4:00 P.M. the next day, Hank staggered into my office in what can most kindly be described as an altered state. His usually immaculate, white Perry Ellis shirt and pale silk Ralph Lauren tie were accessorized with ugly stains of chocolate and raspberry. What appeared to be dandruff on the shoulders of his dark Italian suit turned out on closer inspection to be powdered sugar. The usually haunted, imploring look on his gaunt face was replaced by the fixed, beatific smile of the religious zealot. His eyes and his upper lip had an eerie, glazed look.

With trembling hands he pried open the dozen-count box to reveal only two intact glazed doughnuts and one powdered blueberry-filled doughnut from which a large ragged bite had been wrenched.

Our two right hands shot into the box grabbing both glazed doughnuts.

Hank wolfed his down in one gulp, then studied my face for the telltale signs of Nirvana and caffeine lust.

I was never so acutely disappointed my life. Oh, the glazed doughnut was very fine, a real standout in its genre. But my worst fears were confirmed when I poked an oral thermometer into its side and got a digital readout of just 93.4.

"Dr. London, I know what you're thinking," babbled Hank, defensively holding up six chocolate and four raspberry fingers, "but I was stuck for three hours in traffic coming back and the weather turned cold and my heater went on the fritz."

"In other words, Hank," I observed icily, "these Krispy Kremes have arrived D.O.A. They died of hypothermia and you killed them."

Hank tried to recoup by reserving a weekend suite for my wife and me at the Bellagio in Las Vegas. A complimentary tray of warm Krispy Kremes, fresh from the local franchise, was brought to our room as soon as we arrived. After my first bite, I knew at once why Elvis Presley had become addicted to these Southern delicacies, and why the average body mass index of any community into which Krispy Kremes is introduced shoots up four points per annum.

I love Krispy Kremes, but (sorry, Hank) I still like the other drug.

3

No Wonder They Call It "La Belle Époque"

THE RECENT DEMISE OF THE GORY TWENTIETH CENTURY calls to mind the contrasting euphoria that pervaded America one hundred years ago. Called the "Gay Nineties" in this country, and "La Belle Époque" in Europe, the turn of the last century was a time of untrammeled joy, artistic creation, and exuberant flowerings of intellect.

And no wonder: It was an era when tens of millions of adults and children regularly imbibed cheap home remedies containing small doses of alcohol, cocaine, and morphine. Men built railroads with their bare hands, women raised families of eight without a whimper, and all the babies slept like angels!

Never again will Coca-Cola, now the official soft drink of the World Wide Web, contain actual cocaine as it did when it first went "over the counter" in the early 1900s. Women will no longer enjoy the pinch of opium widely thought to be mixed with pure grain alcohol in Lydia Pinkham's indispensable tonic for "periodic discomfort." Nor will slightly out-of-sorts Londoners in need of a restorative soupçon of laudanum (a tincture of alcohol and opium) be able to nip into the corner chemist for a dram of temporary relief.

Under the influence of their home remedies, agreeably energized, mildly narcotized Americans of the late nineteenth century bound their nation together with railroad tracks and telegraph wires. In the first flush of twentieth-century enlightenment, they installed indoor plumbing and incandescent light fixtures. Like an opium dream, the World's Fair of 1904 transformed St. Louis into Xanadu. Movies of the fair show lean, muscular citizens quickstepping from one spellbinding exhibit to another. This quickstep was not an aberration of early cinematography. It's the way hyped-up Americans moved in those days.

That was then. Look at us now: We're a global community of fat slobs with carpal tunnel syndrome who sit day and night with ample buttocks overflowing our chairs, addictively surfing the Web for video sex, discounted boy toys, vapid chat rooms, hair restorers, penis enhancers, and liver-shriveling nutritional supplements.

During La Belle Époque everyone was mildly and productively stoned on morphine and cocaine offered at cut-rate prices. Nowadays relatively few Americans are affluent enough to contribute countless billions each year to the international relief of Colombian drug lords.

For the masses and the elite the mild doses of narcotics of La Belle Époque have been replaced by overdoses of cyberschlock. The year 2000 found the best and brightest minds of the Western world on St. John's Wort, in artistic limbo, and intellectually dumbed down. In the new millennium the opiate of the masses is the Internet. Millions will log onto Web sites that offer interactive counseling to recovering AOL-coholics.

Sprawled in the doorways of Rodeo Drive, with their six-thousand-dollar linen suits fashionably wrinkled and their repetitively injured hands barely able to grasp their Nokias, the hopelessly stoned, corpulent CEOs of shopping channels and their token husbands will summon chauffeurs to pick them up and shoehorn them back into their ergonomic chairs.

Welcome to La Crummy Époque.

4

Good-bye
Twentieth-Century Stud,
Hello Millennium Man

THE BUZZ OUT OF POWDER ROOMS IN LOS ANGELES, San Francisco, and New York is that the upwardly mobile American woman, seeking a mate whose income at least equals her own, is stuck with a stout, balding gentleman long on manners and short on sexual endowment (due to his enveloping avoirdupois). To put the best face on her limited choices, she is on the lookout for a new millennium Edwardian male.

The instant millionaires of Silicon Valley (an average of sixty-three "born" each day) are suddenly finding themselves eminently eligible as potential mates. As "victims" of their sedentary lifestyles, these overweight and overinformed bachelors are pouring their new wealth into custom tailoring (to cover their paunches) and etiquette lessons (to make up for their having lived as slobs until their IPOs went through the roof).

Stepping from his San Jose mansion and into the backseat of his chauffeur-driven Rolls, the neo-Edwardian discretely squeezes the thigh of his comely blonde companion in anticipation of another night of pricey revelry.

Despite his imposing bulk, the Edwardian man of 1909 was sexually quite frisky, as was the eponymous Edward VII, known to his admirers as "that corpulent voluptuary." After an eight-course dinner at the five-star Connaught Hotel, the Edwardian man-about-town would dash up forty stairs for a two-wench dalliance in his rooms. Truth to tell, current research clearly indicates that a centrally obese man secretes twice as much biologically active testosterone as his skinny counterpart (something to do with insulin resistance).

Attuned to the new zeitgeist, men are putting their dumbbells in mothballs and succumbing to the sedentary charms of rib joints and ice cream parlors. Their universal goal is a body mass index of forty, a normal BMI being twenty-five. Their fixation on toning their pecs, abs, and quads has been replaced by a lust to acquire dewlaps, love handles, and buns of suet.

With the extra hours saved by not having to work out, men are devouring books on elocution. If you can't conquer the ladies with muscle power, the new thinking goes, then subdue them with bright conversation. Women, of course, have always been vulnerable to a man who *talks,* especially one who talks well.

Introducing the neo-Edwardian male.

In their frenzy to affect British accents, today's guys-on-the-make have depleted Blockbuster's entire stock of Olivier's *Hamlet* and Leslie Howard's *Pygmalion.* They are hanging up their sweat suits, jeans, and T-shirts, and donning morning coats, ascots, and plus-fours. Their neatly trimmed beards and mustaches remain in place, but the earrings are gone. Mirror-polished oxfords are in, Nikes, out.

In his rush to embody the current image of the Millennium Man, is the American male endangering his health? Of course he is, and this is where we internists come in. To offset the high LDL cholesterol produced by his Edwardian diet, we simply prescribe Lipitor, Zocor, or some other statin, and throw in an 81 mg. aspirin tablet as a lagniappe.

For the elevated blood sugar associated with his central obesity, we offer a choice of five different diabetic pills that almost certainly, alone or in combination, will allow him to have his cake and eat it too.

Thanks to side effects from all this medication, the neo-Edwardian, unlike his 1909 counterpart, will undoubtedly suffer erectile dysfunction.

So that he can maintain a stiff upper lip during an Edwardian evening of slap and tickle, we, of course, will dole out Viagra.

The less than affluent American guy-on-the-make is viewing this paradigm shift of desirable male traits with alarm. The buff, cookie-cutter FedEx driver with big hair and large appendage is suddenly seeing an endangered species staring back at him from his full-length bathroom mirror.

In the not too distant past, the American man in the street—and who can argue that a FedEx driver is *not* an American man in the street?—collectively spent billions on refoliating his scalp and surgically enhancing his breeding tube. He is now frantically seeking out surgeons newly skilled at uprooting and downsizing.

One plastic surgeon, who chooses anonymity, says he essentially uses the same technique on the outsized penis that he employs in rhinoplasty. "The patient ends up with a schvantz shaped like Errol Flynn's schnoz, minus one nostril. It's really quite svelte."

As with any mass enthusiasm, the avid female pursuit of the Edwardian male is already beginning to run out of steam. A few women are starting to ask themselves, "Is a fat, balding, impotent fop who never shuts up really what I want?"

This is the kind of question that can incite a backlash. If I were a young guy with an eye for the ladies, I'd be thinking of hanging up my morning coat and removing the mothballs from my jock strap before it's too late.

5

Surgeons and Hugh Hefner Wear Pajamas All Day, but Surgeons Have More Fun

I KNOW A GENERAL SURGEON WHO, before he eats a bacon, lettuce, and tomato sandwich, dissects it. This evisceration of an American classic by a thin, balding surgeon in his late fifties is a daily ritual in the doctors' dining room of our local hospital. (The doctors' dining room, off the main cafeteria, is a little elitist thing that allows the surgeon to cut up and the internist to wind down without wearing their real or assumed masks.)

Before the dissection begins, Dr. Bacon, as I will call him, drapes his section of the table with a reasonably sterile napkin. Choosing sharp and blunt instruments from the cafeteria tray, he then unroofs the BLT and carefully lays aside the top sections of toast. With another napkin handed to him by an intern seated to his right, he sponges up the excess mayonnaise adhering to the cross-sections of exposed, blood-red tomatoes.

Grasping two forks, he retracts the fibrous lettuce leaves, and then teases apart the tangle of bacon. With deft scalpel work (for which he uses a steak knife), he cuts away the fatty plaques from each strip of bacon.

Having excised two hundred life-threatening calories from his BLT, Dr. Bacon turns to the intern and says, "Melvin, would you close, please?"

The intern rather clumsily reassembles the sandwich, which the wiry surgeon, suddenly in a hurry, proceeds to devour in four cheek-ballooning bites. "Oops," he mumbles, as some of the reconstructed sandwich oozes out and dribbles onto his lap. (When this happens to me, I perform an emergency laparotomy on my gray flannel slacks to save a huge cleaning bill. Surgeons, wisely, wear their scrubs to lunch.)

As far as I'm concerned, Dr. Bacon is entitled to his eccentricities since surgeons lead a much more harrowing life than other doctors. Once Dr. Bacon appeared in the doctor's dining room trembling just after a difficult case. Out of the clear blue, he turned to me and accusingly cried, "You internists have *no* idea what we go through!"

Actually, I do.

During my internship I saw enough going on inside an operating room to drive me into the safer confines of an internist's office. While the internist feverishly explores his sample drawer for a corticosteroid cream to treat his patient's stubborn rash, the surgeon is trying to find the bleeder that's filled his patient's abdominal wound with blood. The more vital the organ they specialize in, the more I hold the surgeon in awe. I prostrate myself before the brain surgeon. I merely nod to the prostate surgeon.

As an intern I once assisted a neurosurgeon by pressing a foot pedal on his command to activate an electro-coagulator. For twelve hours he used the spark I generated to stop the bleeding from a teenage boy's tumorous brain. Every minute or so he would signal me in his calm Southern accent, "Fry me, Doctah."

During the thirteenth hour, with his tumor almost fully removed, the patient died on the operating table. When attempts at resuscitation failed, the surgeon's bright-pink forehead above his mask broke out in a sweat and turned chalk-white. He stripped off his gloves and quietly asked me to close the incision in the dead boy's scalp while he stepped outside to talk to the anxious family.

During one of his sandwich dissections, Dr. Bacon reminded me, "Oscar, a surgeon's all alone in the OR and there's no one to help him out if he gets into trouble."

"What about your assistant surgeon and all those nurses and techs?" I asked.

"That's all they are—assistants. When something horrible and unexpected happens in the OR, as it does to even the best surgeons, you and you alone must try to get the patient out of there alive. The reason I'm one of the top surgeons in town," said Dr. Bacon modestly, "is that I handle chaos better than most of my colleagues."

"We internists are no strangers to chaos," I pointed out.

"Yeah, but when you eggheads get into trouble, you pick up a phone and page a cardiologist or a pulmonary guy. There's no master surgeon around to help me when I'm in over my head."

"So that's why you surgeons retire much younger than we internists do," I said. "It's stress. I always thought it was because you made so much dinero that you could afford to bail out sooner."

"In spite of the stress, we surgeons love our job. If things go well in the OR, as they usually do, it's like winning the Super Bowl and the World Series on the same day. In our dressing rooms we talk about our cases like a bunch of fighter pilots after a dogfight. Before managed care, we used to make a *lot* more dough than you thinkers and dreamers did, and we *earned* it."

"How do you manage to survive," I asked, "when the patient under your knife doesn't?"

"If I can convince myself that I did my best, I can go on. There's not a night I go to bed after an operation that I don't worry myself to sleep over there possibly being a bleeder I missed."

Through the decades in which I've practiced internal medicine, Dr. Bacon and his surgical colleagues have earned my admiration. I love what the British humorist Evelyn Waugh said when he learned that his good friend Randolph Churchill, the brilliant but very difficult son of Winston, had a benign tumor removed from his lung: "Leave it to the surgeons to find the only thing that was benign in Randolph," observed Waugh, "and remove it."

With his meticulous way about a BLT sandwich and his agony of self-doubt at night, Dr. Bacon epitomizes what I would want my own surgeon to be. That is, if, God forbid, I had to turn over one of my vital organs to a masked and gowned member of the Secret Society.

In sum, I would allow my own surgeon to indulge every one of his or her eccentricities as long as they remained neatniks and worrywarts in the OR and limited their substance abuse to BLT sandwiches. Furthermore, my very own eviscerator must have the eyes of an eagle, the hands of a woman, and a vocabulary that does not contain the word "oops."

6

What's That Funny Smell, Doctor?

AFTER EXAMINING PATIENTS AT CLOSE QUARTERS for the past thirty-eight years, I've developed a professional aloofness to disagreeable smells. The ability of doctors to get their job done in the face of noxious odors is one of the things that separate them from other professionals with the exception of garbage collectors, sewer workers, pig farmers, and rest-room attendants.

Whether it's unwrapping a bandage from a gangrenous foot or having to manually disimpact a severely constipated patient, we docs deny ourselves the luxury of wrinkling our nose and flashing the "Q sign"—dropping one's head to the side, with closed eyes and protruding tongue. (Guaranteed crowd-pleaser.)

Walking into certain nursing homes presents some of our biggest olfactory challenges. The nursing homes are largely filled with patients whose objectionable odors prompted their families to kick them out of the house and into a "home." The advancement of a civilization is proportionate to its ability to suppress bodily odors. During the reign of Louis XIV, Paris stank to high heaven, but elegant Versailles featured L'Orangerie, a cluster of blossoming orange trees grown around the royal latrine, presaging Glade and other air fresheners.

The office practice of internal medicine is, for the most part, odor-free. Patients who make routine appointments to see me usually take the trouble to shower first and sometimes apply cologne or perfume. As a doctor, you may be able to withstand the sight of blood without fainting, but if you can't stand a whiff of cologne or perfume you have no business in office medicine.

I've always suspected surgeons of being averse to bottled scents; otherwise why would anyone choose to spend his or her professional life covering their nose with a mask in an air-purified room?

Some ethnogeographic observations I've made about fresh versus odiferous patients in my multicultural practice: With a few pungent exceptions, the freshest ones are American citizens of any ethnic background. The worst offenders are white European males, including British males.

Do these people bathe? Do they launder their shirts and dry-clean their suits? I don't think so. Overseas they share a common currency, to accompany their common stench. If the European economy continues to boom, these men will give new meaning to the term "stinking rich." When they get around to laundering their money, I can only hope they'll throw in their undies as well.

Last week a twenty-three-year-old Hungarian exchange student came to my office with fever, sore throat, and a body odor that could empty the Louisiana Super Dome on Super Bowl Sunday. Running an hour late, as I often do, I could smell him long before I could see him.

My secretary, Susan, kept wrinkling her nose and flashing me the Q sign as she frantically pointed her thumb toward Exam Room Three at the end of the hall. She had already filled the rest of the office with toxic clouds of room spray. "Please, see him now," Susan begged, "so we can put him behind us and get on with the rest of our lives!"

Finally relenting, I opened the door of Exam Room Three and felt literally shoved backward by the oppressive vapors emanating from the body of the unkempt young man. He was seated next to his immaculately scrubbed and groomed American girlfriend, who tenderly held his fevered hand. I had always known that love was blind; here was a case of love being anosmic as well—meaning she'd lost her sense of smell.

While I breathed through my mouth, the patient began an elaborate introduction in very broken English, which I cut short with a curt wave of my hand. I gestured for him to sit on the exam table where I quickly examined his throat—a textbook case of strep tonsillitis and terminal halitosis.

With his companion's help, I informed him that he needed ten days of penicillin, lots of fluids, and a lifetime supply of antiperspirant. Since there appeared to be no Hungarian word for antiperspirant, I picked up my prescription pad and sketched, for his edification, a cylinder of deodorant with roll-on ball.

When I handed him my drawing, he blushed a deep crimson and muttered a few angry words to his girlfriend. She also blushed and told me that he thought I'd drawn a picture of a penis and just what was I trying to tell him?

When they finally left the office, Susan and I flung open every window in the place and emptied three cans of room spray. It was too late. Cecile, my thirteen-year-old goldfish in Exam Room Three, lay belly-up in her tank.

The coroner said it was the room spray.

7

The Celebrity Patient:
A Doctor's Curse

ALL MY PATIENTS ARE VIPs, except the celebrities.

At first, you're flattered. Eldora Mae Downy, asking *me* to be her doctor! In literary circles, she's a household word—not to be confused with the fabric softener of the same name.

Thirty years ago I had devoured Ms. Downy's novels of young American expats in Paris and Venice during the early fifties, lusting after wealth, fame, and each other. When I first met her last year, she didn't look anything like the picture on the dust jackets of her still-in-print books. After thirty years, thanks to plastic surgery, she looked much younger.

As a twenty-three-year-old author, haggard from writing eighteen hours a day, she wanted to appear on the dust jacket looking more mature than her years. Unlike what she told her plastic surgeon thirty years later, she'd instructed the dust-jacket photographer not to remove any blemishes and frown lines. The photographer overachieved.

Being driven to my office in her black Mercedes and asked by seven patients in my waiting room for her autograph, she'd clearly achieved wealth and fame. And by the looks of her, eternal youth.

When, in a slurred, whiskey-baritone voice, she shouted briefly into her Nokia at her boyfriend in Rome, I realized she hadn't quite obtained all she'd lusted for. After we introduced ourselves in my consultation room, she dimpled seductively and asked me if she could smoke. I reluctantly declined and her surgically enhanced smile froze.

So, after all my anticipation of meeting her, I was stuck with a cigarette and alcohol addict who was unlucky in love. For starters.

On our first visit, she asked (1) if I could write Alitalia a note medically excusing her from flying to Rome the following week, (2) if I could fill out a form for a permanent handicapped placard for her Mercedes, and (3) if I had any samples of Valium?

Oh boy.

When I asked her what medications, if any, she was taking, she motioned to her long-suffering personal secretary, "Ms. Teasedale," a young woman of twenty-seven who looked eighty-three. Ms. Teasedale opened a Vuitton leather case stamped with her boss's gold monogram and dumped at least seventy plastic pill containers onto the wooden counter of the exam room. The clatter sounded like a ten-second excerpt from *Riverdance*.

"Ms. Downy will need five refills of all of these," announced Ms. Teasedale.

Twelve of the empty bottles were labeled "Vicodin," seven "Valium," thirteen "Nembutal," and eleven "Dexedrine Spansules." More than thirty empty containers were labeled in French, German, and Spanish.

I turned in astonishment toward Ms. Downy, who had fallen fast asleep on the exam table, exuding a commingled scent of Chanel No. 5 and Vat 69.

"Jet lag," diagnosed Ms. Teasedale, explaining that the foreign pills were "hormones, rejuvenators, and sexual toners."

"Would you please order the American equivalents?" she asked.

Oy.

I explained to her personal secretary that "Ms. Downy had placed herself in the hands of a doctor who's massively opposed to smoking and the improper use of habit-forming drugs like alcohol, Valium, Vicodin, and God-knows-what."

Narrowing her bloodshot eyes, Ms. Teasedale pointed out, "You wouldn't want Ms. Downy to go into acute withdrawal because you refused to refill her medications, would you?"

I excused myself to retire to my rest room, where I took an emergency Xanax tablet.

Celebrities, at least the few I've dealt with, make terrible patients. They immediately appoint me an honorary member of their entourage, expecting me to satisfy their every medical whim, and to be grateful for my role as their increasingly humble servant.

They pretend to detest their celebrity but secretly love it. Take Woody Allen (not one of my patients). Looking as if they were slept in, those crummy T-shirts and wrinkled pants that are his trademark attire are, in reality, custom-made in quantity and immaculately cleaned. He feigns a passion for anonymity but for years tooled around Manhattan in a gleaming white Rolls-Royce.

Many celebrities, Woody Allen excepted, have turned to euphoriant drugs to maintain the transient, celestial highs they enjoy from a standing ovation of thousands in an auditorium. Or from the enchanted looks of restaurant patrons seated at less prestigious tables.

The late Oscar Levant, professional musician, humorist, and hypochondriac, once recounted his first meeting with Judy Garland, a fellow epic imbiber of tranquilizers and pain pills. "When the two of us hugged," Levant recalled, "it was a defining moment in the history of the pharmaceutical industry." He likened their embrace to the merger of two giant drug cartels. I can imagine Garland-Levant giving our modern Glaxo Wellcome a run for their money.

Elvis Presley, in his later years, was a drug cartel unto himself. But he was never addicted to drugs more than his fans were—and are—addicted to him.

Meanwhile it proved impossible to rouse my own private celebrity, Eldora Mae Downy, from my exam table. In the end it was necessary to hospitalize her for what the tabloids soon conjectured was "drying out" but what the hospital spokesperson said was "exhaustion attendant on her recent travels and lectures abroad."

I was instructed by Ms. Teasedale to admit her to a private room, which almost immediately was filled to its four corners with huge floral tributes from all over the world. That night the patient abruptly awoke from her stupor, looked around, and cried, "Get me out of this goddamn chapel, I'm not dead yet!" Before I could run some liver function tests and get an MRI of her brain, she signed out of the hospital "AMA," against medical advice.

The following day Ms. Teasedale called to remind me, in acid tones, to refill Ms. Downy's medications.

I wasn't about to be seduced or coerced into overprescribing for Ms. Downy, household word or no. The following month—when she still refused to taper her addicting drugs or modify her drinking habits, or join a twelve-step program—I resigned from her case by registered mail.

A few days later Ms. Teasedale phoned me and asked, "Dr. London, would you accept me as your patient? I've also turned in my resignation."

Win some, lose some.

8

Burgers and Fries: The New Weapons of Mass Destruction

WHEN A CHILD DIED LAST YEAR OF AN E. COLI infection from eating an undercooked hamburger at a fast-food restaurant, the media went bananas. As a result millions of pounds of hamburger were impounded. Laws were quickly passed calling for the overcooking of the traditionally overcooked hamburgers at these places. Whew! America was saved from an epidemic of bacterial food poisoning! Excuse me, FDA, it ain't just the bacteria in the burger that's the poison, it's the fat.

I ask you to compare this one tragic death last year with the millions who die young each year from the cardiovascular consequences of eating such food. We tend to wolf down in adulthood those foods we bond with as kids. I myself am doomed, having grown up on all-beef hot dogs and super-thick milk shakes in St. Louis. It took me thirty years to feel comfortable ordering sushi and sashimi. Now that I eat them often, it's too late for my heart—at best, I'll end up with an angioplasty instead of a bypass.

Our kids have been lured into high-fat franchises by the likes of Ronald McDonald, the late Colonel Sanders, a skinny guy named Jack—he of the Styrofoam cranium—and a charismatic Chihuahua. In other words, we have relinquished control of our kids' eating habits to a clown, an airhead, a dead white fat man, and an overbred, under-fed canine.

To the promotional toys these places give away to their young customers, I think it would be appropriate to add purple glucometers and chartreuse blood-pressure cuffs.

While we bomb Iraq for producing weapons of mass destruction, we are, in a sense, guilty of doing the same at home with hamburgers and French fries. Last month a team of UN weapons inspectors raided a caloric bomb factory hidden inside a White Castle in Patterson, New Jersey. They took out thirty-seven cardboard boxes of hamburgers (with onions, mustard, and no pickle) and turned them over to the World Health Organization. After a closed session lasting more than two hours, a WHO spokesperson emerged, burped, and asked, "What hamburgers? Those boxes are empty!"

We are raising a nation of fatties whose exercise consists of moving hand to mouth and hand to mouse. When these roly-poly kids grow up and get jobs, they'll drop dead onto their keyboards in their forties. They'll have to be pried out of their cubicles with the Jaws of Life.

It's obvious to me that the bloated, burger billionaires should direct their charitable funds to the American Heart Association, much as the tobacco execs, out of the goodness of their prosecutors' hearts, are contributing a bundle to lung cancer research.

It's also clear that fast and fat food is here to stay. It's not likely that anytime before the third millennium will we be able to dine at a Tofu Bell.

If your kids insist on going to one of these weapons factories, you can at least demand that they limit their calories and increase their exercise. Since you'll presumably feed them better at home for their next meal, you can give your small fries a small order of fries (210 calories), the smallest hamburger on the menu with mustard instead of the creamy sauce (260 calories), and a small, 80-calorie orange juice. (Calorie counts are based on nutritional data from the Web sites of fast-food companies.)

As role models, we adults must also restrain ourselves inside these places. The good news is that some of the fast-food offerings are delicious and, individually, not that caloric. I say, if you can't beat 'em, eat 'em.

I'm especially fond of the beautifully seasoned potato wedges at KFC (only 180 calories for a small order). They're so tasty that I once schlepped four large orders, deceptively placed in a beautiful, blue Chinese bowl, to an upscale potluck dinner attended by the most educated minds and palates in Berkeley. The potato wedges fooled the executive chef of Berkeley's most famous restaurant, Chez Panisse. (I am not making this up.) He begged me for the recipe.

I was only too happy to direct him to the nearest outpost of the late Colonel's empire. I must say, he took it like a samurai warrior, committing seppuku in one of the eight guest bedrooms. (I am making this part up.)

I defy the most expensive caterer to turn out a more delicious hot hors d'oeuvre than the stuffed jalapeño peppers at Jack-in-the-Box. Filled with molten mozzarella, each large, moderately picante pepper is lightly fried in a delicious crust (560 calories for a "small" order of seven pieces, but my wife and I eat only one each at 75 calories and ask for a doggie bag to feed the rest to El Gordino, our pet Chihuahua).

In the arsenal of edible weaponry, Jack's Bacon Ultimate Cheeseburger (1,150 calories) occupies a special niche. The small community of three thousand souls in the Midwest, which was chosen to test-market the Bacon Ultimate Cheeseburger five years ago, is now a ghost town.

Before invidious comparisons are made to the neutron bomb, which destroys people but leaves buildings intact, it must be pointed out, in all fairness, that shortly after the Bacon Ultimate Cheeseburger was test-marketed, an enormous space ship landed in the town's high school football field.

Lured by a loudspeaker blaring, "Krispy Kremes inside! Come and get 'em!" the entire population of the town disappeared into the bowels of the ship.

So much for the reliability of test-marketing cheeseburgers.

9

For What Will You Be Remembered?

BEFORE WE DIE, many of us want to leave a tangible mark: the four-minute mile, the third-largest ball of string, a .400 batting average, around the world in 25,000 frequent-flyer miles, the Longest Walk on Hands—to each his or her own.

I, of course, will be remembered for the largest number of accumulated hours patients have had to wait to see their doctor during a thirty-five-year practice.

I am not proud of this record, but I've been comforted by the documented observation that patients who are unwilling to wait at least a half-hour to see their doctor die young.

In fact I have hundreds of patients who, if they were ushered into my office to see me two minutes after they arrived, would die of shock. As I indicated in the title of my first book, I make every effort to kill as few patients as possible.

For some reason the Guinness book of records passed me over and cited another doctor, Daniel Carlin, M.D., of Boston, for a different category: "Greatest Distance between Doctor and Patient." Last year, according to the millennial edition of Guinness, Dr. Carlin e-mailed lifesaving advice to Russian yachtsman Victor Yazkov, who was sailing off Cape Town, South Africa, 9,906 miles away.

Big, if I may say, deal. Carlin merely advised Yazkov to lance the boil on his arm and stop taking aspirin to prevent post-op bleeding. What is not recorded is the Greatest Distance a Denial-of-Benefits Form Traveled between an HMO and a Patient when, one conjectures, Dr. Carlin's billing office attempted to collect a fee from Yazkov for the good doctor's service.

One of my patients, Gus LeBrecht (as I'll call him), retired as a parking lot mogul at age fifty-two and spent the next twenty-five years of his life trying to get into the Guinness Book of Records. He may hold the record for the most unsuccessful attempts—307.

A recent example: In the fall of 1997 Gus entered the Fastest Stamp Licker contest and lost by 84 stamps to Diane Sheer of London, who licked and affixed 225 stamps onto envelopes in five minutes (*Guinness World Records 2000*, p. 57).

With gluey lips Gus then stepped across the hall in time to enter the Most People Kissed contest. He started by gallantly bussing his wife and stuck fast. The event was won by Alfred Wolfram, who kissed 11,030 people in eight hours (*Guinness World Records 2000*, p. 50).

Gus and his wife, Marjorie, were inseparable for sixteen hours, far short of the record for Longest Kiss—twenty-nine hours—held by Mark and Roberta Grisworld of Allen Park, Michigan (*Guinness World Records 2000*, p. 50).

In the fall of 1998, Gus collapsed after 315 feet during the annual World Wife-Carrying Championship held in Sinkajarvi, Finland (*Guinness World Records 2000*, p. 57). Not clear on the concept, his wife, Marjorie, ended up carrying Gus over the, uh, Finnish line.

During his last ten years Gus turned his obsessive quest for everlasting fame to downhill skiing. Among aging skiers, two million vertical feet is a shining goal to achieve before they schuss off this mortal coil. It may not be quite worthy of Guinness, but it's a sterling accomplishment.

Last month, against the protests of his long-suffering wife, Marjorie, Gus took up permanent residence in a ski lodge adjacent to the longest downhill course in the world: the Weissfluhjoch-

Kublis Parsenn near Davos, Switzerland (*Guinness World Records 2000,* p. 216).

Marjorie, who is on the short list at Guinness for Longest-Suffering Wife, reluctantly trudged off to the Weissfluhjoch with Gus.

At 7 miles, 1,038 yards per run, Gus was confident of achieving two million vertical feet by January 11, his seventy-fifth birthday.

Alas, on January 10, he died on the slopes just eight vertical feet short of his goal.

Marjorie arranged for Gus to be buried at the foot of the run with his skis alongside him in a grave dug nine feet deep.

Marjorie reminds us that, in the end, all of us will be most remembered not for what we did but for how deeply we loved.

10

Mars and Venus vs. Aesculapius

JAKE LEFKOWITZ, AGE SIXTY-TWO, SLUMPS LIKE A COMMA on the end of the exam table. His thin, gray mustache twitches unhappily. With my back against the door, I stand smiling before him, defeating any notion he might be entertaining of bolting from the room.

Behind him, on a chair against the wall, sits his wife, Sophie, age sixty, with her arms crossed over her ample bosom. Jake is caught between a rock and a hard place. The expression on his face seems to be internally shouting, "How did I wind up in the same room with my two worst enemies?"

"How are you feeling, Jake?" I ask, expecting a half-hour monologue.

"Fine," he answers, nodding.

At this, Sophie, in the background, vigorously shakes her head.

"Uh-oh," I tell myself. "One of these Man-from-Mars-Woman-from-Venus conjugal visits."

"Doc, there's nuttin' wrong with me," the Martian insists.

"What about your hernia!" the Venusian shouts. "Your headaches? Your chest pains? Getting up five times a night to pee! I knew you'd clam up as soon as I dragged you in here!"

"I can't get a word in edgewise," says Jake in a stage whisper. "And she never shuts up."

In the presence of this incarnation of Mars and Venus, I'm thrust into the conciliatory role of Aesculapius, the god of medicine.

"By Jove," I declare, while feeling Jake's left inguinal hernia, "it's high time you had this repaired." Now, it's difficult to argue with Aesculapius, especially when he's got his hand around one of your private parts.

"What do you say, Jake?" I ask. "Let's go for it!"

In a brave act of *lèse-majesté,* Jake shakes his head.

Sophie nods.

"Are your chest pains getting worse?" I ask.

Jake shakes his head. Sophie nods.

"Are you remembering to take your nitroglycerin?"

Male nod, female shake.

"Dr. London," Sophie calls from the rear, "I want you to put Jake in the hospital. He's a sick man. You can ask our son, Gerald."

"What kind of doctor is Gerald?"

"He's not a doctor—he's a lawyer. And he's mad as hell about the lack of care his father's getting."

With this comment Mrs. Lefkowitz has invoked Satan. The god of medicine is forced to appeal to a Higher Authority: I write out an authorization request to Jake's HMO, begging the powers that be to approve my referral of Jake to a surgeon.

In the twelve years that have passed since this clash of the titans, Jake has had his left inguinal hernia repaired (twice), his right coronary artery stented, his prostate gland resected, and his headaches controlled by Imitrex, Maxalt, Zomig, or Amerge, depending on which of these antimigraine miracle drugs Aesculapius has in his sample drawer.

Jake says he now feels wonderful. Through the years Sophie fought him every step of the way until Jake, unlike Sinatra, did it her way.

It's a fact that married men outlive bachelors, and wives survive their husbands. One reason women stick around longer than men is that women, unlike men, aren't afraid of doctors.

For many women their defining medical experience was with their kindly obstetrician in the celebratory ambience of the maternity wing. Women often associate flowers and balloons with doctors.

By contrast, the first significant medical encounter for most men in this country is with the doctor who performed their circumcision. (Thanks to primal scream therapy, I now remember every detail of mine. Don't ask.) Small wonder the next doctor we old boys submit to, albeit unwillingly, is the urologist.

Suddenly we're sixty-two and having to get up five times during the wee-wee hours of the morning. To cure our nocturnal frequency, the urologist offers us a brutal recommendation and no alternatives. Flowers and balloons for the ladies. Knives and catheters for the men.

Between the time we're circumcised and the time we're again penalized, as it were, we guys make strenuous efforts to keep away from doctors. Unless we let our guards down and marry.

I've never seen a husband drag his wife to the doctor. I've seen a thousand wives drag their husbands into my office. As long as the husband can still kick and scream, I have a chance to defer his heart attack or stroke for a decade or two. "First I'm dragged," complained one husband, "then I'm drugged."

And the wives, no matter how cruel their methods of coercion, deserve a great deal of credit for showing love for their husbands this way. Jake and Sophie recently paid a joint visit to my office shortly after their fiftieth wedding anniversary party.

"Thanks to you, Dr. London," said Jake, warmly shaking my hand, "we had a fabulous time!"

In her walker, Sophie stood behind him, pursing her lips and shaking her head.

11

How I Rank My Patients

COLONEL GEORGE H. STANHOPE (U.S. ARMY, RETIRED) began his career in OCS and ended it with OCD. That would be officers' candidate school at Fort Sam Houston, Texas, and obsessive-compulsive disorder in Berkeley, California.

He had the misfortune of serving on the retreating side in two wars, Korea and Vietnam, and as a result, never made general. In my own experience in the military (captain, Army Medical Corps, Okinawa, 1958–60), I never met a general I didn't like or a colonel I did.

Among life's losers, the most difficult to be around are the near-misses, like colonels, vice presidents, and second violinists.

In the military, Stanhope's rank was called "bird" or "chicken" colonel, because of its insignia depicting a spread-winged eagle. By contrast, the mark of the lieutenant colonel (a near-miss, once removed) is a silver maple leaf.

Fifteen years after retirement, George Stanhope still insisted on being called "Colonel." His black cashmere blazer, white shirt, red-white-and-blue bow tie, and khaki pants made up his immaculate retirement uniform. The crease in his pants could cut glass.

In the sandal-wearing town of Berkeley, his black, mirror-polished Florsheims defined him as a man apart.

I once made the mistake of playfully asking him if his rank was technically inferior to that enjoyed by another "chicken colonel," named Sanders, of fast-food fame. Colonel Stanhope was not amused. As penance I asked him to reiterate one of his insufferably boring military anecdotes, with which he obliged me, to my profound regret. (I have spent half my life in medicine at the mercy of monologuists.)

According to Colonel Stanhope, his troops uniformly took top honors during battalion inspections. His men may not have won battles but ranked highest among their peers for neatness of their tents, cleanliness of their mess kits, and depth of shine on their belt buckles.

An officer with an obsessive-compulsive disorder serves with distinction during the long intervals between wars but tends to come unglued in the chaos of battle. I took little comfort in realizing that those under his command who didn't survive died with clean mess kits.

His rigidity of thinking unhappily carried over to his preference for "Southern white boys" under his command. He revealed this predilection in one of his rare, unguarded moments while he was holding forth on his hero, General Robert E. Lee.

"They're the best troops in the world," he claimed. "The Yankees won the War between the States only because their heavy industry was superior to ours."

It will come as no surprise to learn that Colonel Stanhope grew up in Virginia.

You might wonder how this squeaky-clean right-winger came to live in "Stinko, Pinko Berkeley," as he referred to the town in which I had chosen to do my life's work. His first wife having died suddenly during his third year of retirement (while polishing the family silver), he ended up marrying the widow of a distinguished Berkeley professor.

I never understood what the professor's widow, one of my long-term patients, saw in the spit-and-polish Colonel, until I recalled that her late husband, a distinguished anthropologist of primitive cultures, had been a notorious slob, even by Berkeley standards (and those of many other primitive cultures).

The Colonel's almost debilitating obsessive-compulsive disorder may have cost the lives of a number of his troops in the heat of battle but served to save his own in peacetime. His diabetes and hypertension required a rigid weight-reducing program as well as careful records of the highs and lows of his blood sugar and blood pressure.

He lost twenty-eight pounds in four months and maintained an average fasting value of 110 for both his blood sugar and blood pressure. His multicolored graphs of these vital statistics were worthy of a textbook. And most impressive of all, he maintained his weight loss.

When I begrudgingly complimented him for actually following my advice, which almost all my other patients similarly afflicted had ignored, he replied with a thin smile, "Doctor London, an order is an order, even if I receive it from a former instant-captain in the Medical Corps."

Professional restraint prohibited me from telling the Colonel my opinion of his philosophy, until one afternoon when he had been waiting over a half-hour in my crowded waiting room. Through my secretary's window, I watched the impatient Colonel get up from his seat next to an elderly Chinese gentleman, choose a different magazine from the rack, and pointedly sit down in another part of the room.

Suddenly here was my chance to make a statement. I told my secretary that I myself would call in the next patient.

Throwing open the door to my waiting room, I stood at attention, and called out, "GENERAL LEE, would you come in please?"

As the Colonel's face turned a fiery red, representing a threat to his scrupulously controlled blood pressure, I ushered in former General Yung Tao Lee of Chiang Kai-Shek's Nationalist Chinese Army.

General Lee had always insisted I call him "Mister Lee." But choosing to address this commanding officer in a losing war by his superior rank, I awarded him at least one small victory, however belated and unwitting.

"Colonel Stanhope," I announced, twisting the knife, "you're next."

12

The Big Apple Goes Organic:
Alternative Medicine Blooms
in Manhattan

Four good-looking, glassy-eyed alternative therapists stare out from the cover of a recent issue of *New York* magazine. A startling caption below their portrait states, "New York has replaced California as the mecca of alternative medicine."

As a Berkeley internist openly fighting the California brand of alternative medicine for thirty-eight years, I felt a transient flush of triumph. I had finally succeeded in driving the quacks out of the Golden State! But no, the therapists on the cover are an indigenous bunch of New York "healers" whose illustrious and wealthy clientele bear out my contention that alternative medicine is a disease of the rich and famous.

According to the article, Dr. Howard Bezoza, a forty-seven-year-old physician trained as a conventional M.D., has several illuminated glass boxes of gorgeous crystals embedded in the walls of his "center." (By contrast, I have many deep forehead indentations embedded in the walls of my small office; I add a new one each time I'm asked to fill out a form begging an HMO to approve a bone densitometry for one of my patients.) Dr. Bezoza attributes his trim figure to his ingesting plant-based testosterone, obviously unaware of recent studies implicating such "nutritional supplements" in the transmogrification of human testicles into Mexican yams.

Citing a Harvard study, Dr. Bezoza points out, "There's as much money being spent out of pocket on alternative remedies as there is being spent by third-party insurers."

That translates to a fortune for the Bezozas of this country and peanuts for the Bozos like me. Who seeks alternative remedies? "The smartest, most successful people," says the orange-haired, bulging-eyed Bezoza. "So we can't continue to proselytize this issue of the quack!" (As if smart, successful people are immune to the charms of a quack.)

To get an appointment with Dr. Bezoza, you have to wait at least two months or be referred by a VIP. A cash-only operation, each session usually runs $250 to $300 plus the cost of supplements and infusions. By contrast you must wait forty-eight hours to see me. If you announce that a VIP has referred you, my secretary will laugh raucously and slam down the phone in your ear. In my office a session runs between $5 and $10 depending on the size of your HMO copayment, plus a $6 outlay to your pharmacist for each of my HMO-approved generic medications whose side effects will drive you to the door of Dr. Bezoza, if you can get in. (Tell his secretary Oscar sent you.)

Dr. Bezoza's patients may be well heeled, but are they healed well?

Nina Burleigh, the author of the cover article, visited the hallowed premises of the Bezoza Center, where, "Down one hall, a woman snoozes in a recliner, covered with a plaid blanket, her arm attached to an IV delivering a yellowish liquid into her vein . . . a vitamin infusion, a specialty of the house." If a Nobel Prize for chutzpah is ever awarded, it will go to Dr. Bezoza unless he has discovered, in his yellowish liquid, a new way to deliver chicken soup.

Dr. Robert Atkins, sixty-eight, the famous author of high-protein and low-carbohydrate diet books, runs a seven-story facility of "complementary medicine" on 55th Street in Manhattan. Says Dr. Atkins, "West Coast doctors are more vegetarian, and most of us here are more carnivorous."

I'm also sixty-eight, an author of medical books, but I never prescribe the Atkins diet. I rent eight hundred square feet of office space from two carnivorous landlords in a small, two-story medical building. What am I doing wrong?

Dr. Ron Hoffman practices both traditional and alternative medicine in Manhattan. "There's a big difference in the style of the New York alternative practitioners compared with their West Coast colleagues," he says. "Some are doing the touchy-feely spiritual stuff, but there is a more hard-assed approach here. In California, it's more of an aesthetic thing."

In my humble opinion the reason the New York alternative therapists are more hard-assed than their California colleagues is all that animal protein in the Atkins Diet.

Striking a fair balance, the *New York* magazine article cites one of my heroes, Wallace Sampson, M.D., a Stanford professor of clinical medicine and former chairman of the National Council for Reliable Health Information. This group sees almost no medical advantage to any of the alternative offerings. Moreover, the article points out, the council blames the cultural relativism of the sixties for infecting medicine with pseudoscience. "I see no benefit to any of it," Sampson says.

Dr. Sampson has a theory about how the alternative medicine virus entered the culture. "Harvard offered courses, and then the hospitals in New York started doing it. These programs are set up by rich people with an ideological agenda that nature is good and science and technology are bad, that truth is a relative, culturally determined thing, so that science is diminished. There will be a price to pay for this later on, in terms of health and the indoctrination of medical students."

I hope Sampson never gets a haircut.

13

Om Sweet Om

PATIENTS FREQUENTLY ASK ME, "Where do you get all your energy?" No one ever asked me that question at age eighteen. As a teenager, I suffered from what is now called "chronic fatigue syndrome" but was then referred to as "goofing off." Fifty years later I can thank the feisty genes of my mother, who died at ninety-four, and the bliss of centuries-old meditation for my heightened energy. ("Uh-oh, London's going touchy-feely on us.")

Meditation is my one deep bow to alternative medicine. I learned the technique thirty years ago from a true believer in Transcendental Meditation who put me through a mildly embarrassing ceremony that culminated in my ruining a perfectly good handkerchief and being assigned an unlisted mantra.

I never subscribed to the spiritual or communal aspects of TM, but the simple technique, adapted by Herb Benson in his bestseller *The Relaxation Response,* has always appealed to me. The TM people were last heard from trying to levitate from a futon on a hardwood floor, using their gluteus and hamstring muscles. I repaid my old TM mentor by treating his severely pulled hamstrings free of charge and free of smirk.

My mantra worked the first time I tried it. And it has ever since. The only spiritual quality I bring to meditation is that I practice it, religiously, twice a day, without fail. I use it solely to step away from the world for twenty minutes before and after work.

Just sitting in a comfortable chair and breathing in and out appealed to the feckless eighteen-year-old in me from the start. It's great getting out of bed in the morning and then doing nothing. As you breathe out, you say your mantra to yourself. It doesn't take a rocket scientist or a neurosurgeon to learn how to meditate, but these are exactly the types of highly stressed professionals who should meditate but don't.

I've tried to persuade my overworked patients to try it, but they soon drop out for a lack of compulsiveness, which is a trait I have in spades. (If your doctor isn't compulsive, find one who is.)

Doing it for decades has probably resulted in my being addicted to meditation. When I'm kept from meditating at my usual time, which happens rarely, I actually feel withdrawal anxiety. Then, as soon as I'm able to tune in my mantra, the bliss kicks in and all's well with the world. I define the bliss I feel as "the sound of no phone ringing."

When my daughter Jenny was seven and easily frightened, she observed me hanging upside down in my space boots for ten minutes each evening, then solemnly disappear inside my den. One night she ran up to her mother and asked with trembling lips, "Is Daddy a vampire?" To this day my wife insists she merely replied, "No, darling." Jenny recalls the additional words, "Not exactly."

One of the problems I've had with meditation is finding the proper place. My office and home are not ideal because that's where the phones are. The hospital just up the street has a small, nondenominational chapel, which would be perfect except that I have to share it with people who use the sanctuary of the chapel to cheat on their diets.

These closet gluttons huddle in the darkest corner of the chapel and painstakingly unwrap their candy bars and Doritos Nacho Cheese Chips. The deafening crinkle of paper drowns out my mantra. Even God cannot hear the prayers of the few devout chapel-goers through all that crackly static from the back of the chapel.

41

No, that temporary bulge in the side pocket of my navy blue blazer is not a bag of Doritos. Rather, Cheetos. I've given up on the chapel as conducive to meditation. I say, if you can't lick 'em, munch 'em.

Last Sunday afternoon I found the ideal venue. I was on weekend call for six practices including my own. My pocket pager was vibrating so often that for hours after I unhooked it from my belt on Saturday night I felt phantom vibrations in my right hip.

Sunday afternoon was brutal. I admitted three patients through the ER (myocardial infarction, stroke, and aspiration pneumonia). Then dashed over to the Shattuck Theater in downtown Berkeley to join my wife and daughter for a 3:00 P.M. screening of *The Buena Vista Social Club*. This is the much-heralded documentary about six elderly, once-famous Cuban musicians rescued from obscurity by Wim Wenders, the film's director.

The downtown parking crunch took eight days off my life expectancy until I found a place six blocks from the theater. I half-walked, half-jogged to the multiplex. I arrived at a quarter past three and found no wife and daughter. I bought my ticket for Theater 3, assuming they had gone inside, and discovered to my vast relief that the film would actually start at 4:00 P.M. I had gotten the time wrong.

Uncharacteristically I had forty-five minutes to kill. My pager vibrated and by the time I mollified the caller (an elderly man who was afraid he'd taken too much milk of magnesia by mistake—an error that Mother Nature would soon rectify), I was down to thirty-nine minutes. A sudden, overwhelming urge to meditate stole over me. But there was no place to sit down in the lobby.

Cautiously I peeked inside the door of Theater 3 and gasped.

I was instantly reminded of the most famous moment in the history of archeology when Howard Carter broke the seal of King Tut's tomb and peered inside the vault by candlelight. He saw all kinds of strange objects that had not seen light for three thousand years. Everywhere he looked was the glint of gold.

His friend, Lord Carnarvon, asked, "Do you see anything?"

"Yes," replied Carter. "Wonderful things."

Before I tell you what I saw, you must know that the Shattuck

Theater was recently remodeled to resemble the great art deco movie palaces of the thirties. An Egyptian theme ran through many of these awesome theaters. With plaster statues painted gold and carvings inlaid with glass jewels, the Shattuck has lovingly re-created the pharaohs, temples, and tombs of Ancient Hollywood.

When I peered inside the door to Theater 3, I too saw wonderful things, namely 150 empty seats surrounded by gold and crimson Egyptian artifacts. Suffused with a soft, Viagra-blue light, the temporarily vacated theater was as quiet as a tomb.

Brimming with anticipation, I took an aisle seat in the twelfth row, closed my eyes, and plunged into my mantra. As sometimes happens, I dove too steeply, dropped below my mantra, and fell into a deep sleep.

Twenty minutes later I was startled awake by a rude shoving of my left shoulder and the vigorous mussing of my hair. For a moment I thought I was being attacked by a hostile usher, but it was only my wife and daughter waking the pharaoh—or the vampire—from the dead.

14

The Perfect Patient

WITH SOME PATIENTS, IT SEEMS, a doctor can do no wrong. And with others, it's quite the opposite.

Last month I saw a fifty-four-year-old travel writer for the first time. With his completely white hair, somber mien, and protruding abdomen, he looked like Steve Martin with central obesity. I will call him Jim Painter. His first words to me were, "I want to die."

When I asked him why, he said, "My great years are behind me. I've had terminal writer's block for six months, I'm separated from wife, I've gained forty pounds in six months, and I can't stop crying and smoking and drinking. I've got nothing to live for."

After conceding, sadly, that that was a pretty good answer to my question, I asked him if any member of his family had been depressed. "My Dad hanged himself, my older brother shot himself, and my mother, who's physically as healthy as a horse, has sat in a nursing home for six years, refusing medication and waiting to die."

"I suppose you've had a go at psychotherapy."

"Jungian, Freudian, behavior modification, and cognitive therapy with the best. Believe me, nothing works."

"What about antidepressive medications?"

"Prozac, Zoloft, Paxil, Serzone, Wellbutrin, Remeron, Nortriptyline, Parnate, and Effexor. Each taken for at least six weeks. Each made me feel worse than the one I took before."

Suddenly feeling out of my depth, I paddled for shore with a simpler group of questions about his health.

It turned out he suffered from severe acid reflux, allergic rhinitis, and erectile dysfunction. The laboratory tests I had him take before his visit showed a low HDL cholesterol, a high LDL cholesterol, high triglycerides, and a blood sugar of 157, indicating mild diabetes. My physical exam revealed moderate hypertension, slightly wheezy lungs, and a somewhat rapid but regular heartbeat. His EKG was borderline abnormal.

His cluster of hypertension, diabetes, central obesity, high triglycerides, and low HDL cholesterol qualified him for a deadly diagnosis of "Syndrome X." All the abnormalities of Syndrome X stem from insulin resistance and unless treated vigorously, beginning with a crash diet, he would die soon. On his death certificate, "X" would mark the spot.

The only reason this man was still alive, I concluded, was that his body had not been able to decide whether to use a heart attack, stroke, or suicide to wind things up.

At the end of the hour, Jim asked, "What do you think?" Given so many leads, I hardly knew where to begin. I chose to start with the number one organ in the body: the brain.

"First of all, Mr. Painter," I said, "I'm encouraged by your choosing to see a doctor rather than letting things continue to deteriorate. Let's start with your mood. One thing I've learned after thirty-eight years of seeing patients in Berkeley is that mood is chemical. As you've probably learned, no therapist is going to be able to talk you out of your depression. I'm glad you've been open to the biochemical approach."

"But I burned that bridge after Effexor did nothing for me. As you know, I've tried them all and nothing worked."

"The two things you haven't tried are amphetamines and electroshock therapy."

He visibly recoiled at these last words, but rallied to say, "Amphetamines? Speed? Are you serious? I thought amphetamines were pushed by doctors for attention defect disorder and by dealers for getting high."

"Right. But I found out thirty-five years ago, largely through serendipity, that amphetamines can also help a severe depression unresponsive to everything else in the *Physicians' Desk Reference.*"

It took a good deal of verbal arm wrestling on my part in the next ten minutes to persuade Jim to at least try an amphetamine. "If this stuff works," I promised, "you're going to feel the difference with the first pill. You'll be happier and your appetite will diminish. And I'm not talking placebo effect. On the other hand, an amphetamine might just make you more jumpy."

Obviously disappointed in me, he reluctantly pocketed my prescription for Dexedrine Spansule, 15 mg., once daily in the morning, and slouched out of my office in a convincing impersonation of the expression "Dead Man Walking."

As instructed, he called me the next day just before noon. With his first words—"I'll be goddammed"—I knew I had hit pay dirt.

The Dexedrine worked so well in the ensuing weeks that I was able to persuade him to try other, more predictably beneficial medications: a proton pump inhibitor for his acid reflux, an ACE-inhibitor for his hypertension, Glucophage for his diabetes, high-dose niacin for his lipid abnormalities, a corticosteroid nasal spray for his allergic rhinitis, and Viagra for his erectile dysfunction. Everything improbably worked exactly like the drug retail reps promised they would, and then some.

With his continued improvement, I persuaded him to do the impossible: give up smoking, maintain a low-calorie diet, reduce his alcohol intake to two drinks a day, and resume the gym-based exercise routine he had abandoned shortly after his wife left him. Thanks to his being obsessive enough to implement all my advice, his hypertension, diabetes, rhinitis, and acid reflux disappeared, he lost forty pounds, he reversed all his lipid abnormalities, and he reunited with his wife in all the important ways, with an assist from Viagra.

A month after he saw me, his writer's block had evaporated like dry ice on a hot tin roof. His book on the attractions of Northern California will be published next spring.

Jim Painter is one of those rare patients for whom I can do no wrong. Thanks largely to the Mozarts and Shakespeares who created the wonder drugs now available, I've been able to help—really help— more people in the last five years than I did in the previous thirty-three. Even an old drug like Dexedrine—formerly used to wake up patients with narcolepsy—can be a wonder drug for depression.

Who says you can't teach an old drug new tricks?

15

Physicians as Magicians

WHEN I STARTED PRACTICING MEDICINE thirty-eight years ago, doctors were still thought to perform magic. In our invisible black capes, we young docs never met a spirochete of syphilis we couldn't zap with penicillin—astounding! We could press our stethoscopes against a chest for a moment and sagely proclaim, "Aortic regurgitation"—uncanny!

Some of this mojo rubbed off on us from our shamanic ancestors. Before the miracle of antibiotics, a magical aura was about all doctors had going for them. Nowadays as I draw the curtain around the bed of a young hospital patient, the scene resembles the final moments of *The Wizard of Oz*. The patient's family asks, "Who is that old man behind the curtain?" The older I get, the less impressed people seem to be with a doctor's magical aura.

The doctor may be in, but the Wizard is out.

Where did he go? The spirit of the supernatural has fled the cold, sterile hospital room and now resides in the warm, organic tent of the alternative therapist. These "charismapractors," as I call them, have stolen our thunder. With supreme confidence in the validity of their methods, they live off the power of the placebo and the laying-on of hands. Their patients worship them.

I think the reason for this shift of therapeutic magic is that, today, traditional medicine is viewed as a science and alternative medicine as a religion. Too bad. As I see it, only people with high intelligence and minimal gullibility can appreciate the truly magical qualities of traditional medicine as practiced in the new millennium.

Case in point: In 1998, the Swedish Academy of Science awarded the Nobel Prize to three investigators whose work on nitric oxide led to the discovery of the wonder drug Viagra. The male members of this august body pulled off a feat of magic of their own when, while still seated, they gave the three recipients a standing ovation.

For office patients it's necessary to overlook crowded waiting rooms, frowning, overworked doctors, and receptionists with hair-trigger tempers to appreciate the magic a well-trained physician can still bring off diagnostically and therapeutically in this age of managed care.

I myself am in awe of modern medicine. The MRI is a miracle of diagnosis—it reveals curable diseases in the brain that in past years only removal of the skull was able to show. Soon we'll be able to do your colonoscopy using a high-tech CT scanner without having to insert a tube in your rectum. Can a painless mammogram be far behind?

We take for granted much of the magic of medicine. Like once-famous villains, a number of notorious diseases have been driven into obscurity by traditional medicine. What ever happened to smallpox? Gone from the face of the earth! And, except for a relatively few victims each year, polio is a has-been in the first world. Miraculous.

Tuberculosis and syphilis—the AIDS of their heyday—have been chased underground by magic potions called antibiotics. And thanks to the incredibly sophisticated antivirals that continue to be invented, AIDS patients who were consulting their lawyers a few years ago to make out their barely living wills are now sitting down with their travel agents to talk about tropical getaways.

My groaning arthritic patients used to get around on their damaged joints like rusting 1950 Chevrolets in rural Honduras. Now, with arthroplasty, they can trade in their broken-down joints for shiny, metallic models that run like brand-new Audi TT coupes.

Until a few years ago enchanted heart patients used to brag about their five-vessel bypass surgery (which not so incidentally caused a significant amount of mild to moderate brain damage). Now the nonsurgical cardiologist, with the hands of a magician, is threatening to put the surgeon out of business. These dextrous docs are inserting "stents" (firm, hollow tubes) into narrow portions of arteries without having to open the patient's chest. Like building a ship in a bottle, the cardiologist threads the stent through a narrow catheter inserted into a groin artery. After a safe, ninety-minute procedure, these patients emerge with the coronary circulation of hearts twenty years younger. Then they get up from the table and drive home. Sheer magic.

I try my best not to disappoint patients who still expect a little magic in their doctor's office. I may not have a white rabbit in my black bag, but for my heartburn sufferers I do have a little purple capsule called Prilosec that feels like a miracle cure. And I get fan letters from patients whose chronically drippy noses magically dried up when they began using Flonase or other corticosteroid nasal sprays.

Unfortunately the pharmaceutical companies are intruding on my magic by advertising some of these wonder drugs directly to the consumer via TV and print ads. Having seen a blissful married couple in a TV commercial funded by Pfizer, many of my male patients are demanding Viagra samples. With Viagra they hope to perform levitation, that most difficult of illusions, in the privacy of their domestic domiciles. And—*abracadabra!*—one hour after taking Viagra, they've erected a Pfizer high-riser in their bedrooms.

Although I used to receive unfair credit for the magic of a medication, I'm now reduced to the role of the pretty magician's assistant while Pfizer the Fantastic, dressed in corporate top hat and tails, takes all the bows.

Call me a Harried Houdini.

Of course, there's a limit to how much a physician can be a magician. When the Great Zandini saws the pretty lady in half, she comes out whole. I leave that particular trick to my fast-handed colleagues in surgery.

When you come to me, I'd like you to pick a disease, any disease, *but don't tell me what it is.* Alas, thanks to the Internet, now my patients tell *me* what their disease is. More often than not, they're wrong, and if they don't get the disease right, certainly the treatment their Web site instructs me to give them is also wrong. The Internet is a magician's wardrobe trunk bulging with medical wisdom and convincing quackery.

Perhaps modern doctors will enhance their magical role by becoming Wizards of Cyberspace, helping their patients sort out the elusive wisdom from the ubiquitous schlock. For example, Zoloft works wonders for depression. St. John's Wort doesn't.

And for my next illusion, ladies and gentlemen....

16

A Ghastly Reunion
in Room 479

EVERY YEAR ABOUT THIS TIME, when our local hospital census is low, the ghosts of all the people who've died in Room 479 throw a cocktail party. Room 479, at the end of the hall, is where the terminal patients are moved to before they die.

The reason I know about this postmortem reunion is that my latest patient to occupy (and somehow survive) Room 479 recently confided in me, "I swear to God, Dr. London, there were hundreds of them streaming in and out of my room all night."

For the record, my middle-aged, female informant had been on a morphine drip the night of the party. She claimed that the elderly, semitransparent wraiths were still dressed in their skimpy hospital gowns.

They floated in and out of Room 479 all night, reminiscing about their final days and sipping bubbly citrate of magnesia, a laxative, from champagne glasses.

When my informant asked one of them, an old gentleman, why citrate was their drink of choice, he replied, "It actually tastes quite good and the beautiful part of being dead is that there's nothing for it to work on. It causes a little expulsion of inoffensive gas and we use that to move about."

"Thanks to that laxative," recalled my informant, "it wasn't long before all the ghosts were three sheets to the wind."

Another apparition told her, "Night after night you could die waiting for the nurse to come in with a sleeping pill, and I finally did."

Another claimed, "I was doing fine as long as they were giving me another patient's medication by mistake. When I finally pointed this out, I realized I should have kept my mouth shut. As soon as they started treating me with my own doctor's prescriptions, I promptly died. I wish I'd gotten the name of that other patient's doctor. He was terrific!"

Dr. Abner Fenway, as I will call him, was singled out for particular abuse by several former patients. Apparently this distinguished geriatrician's biggest sin was his permanent grin, compounded by his ill-fitting dentures.

"Here I was, dying," complained one female ghost, "and Fenway kept smiling and clacking. On my last day I died five times, and five times he jump-started me with his electric paddles. Finally I looked up and saw that fifty-four-tooth grin of his and, so help me, his toupee was smoking! I mustered all my strength for my last words, 'Do Not Resuscitate.'"

Deceased patients, it would appear, have little respect for their doctors. Curious.

One ghostly geezer carped, "When I died, all that was left for me to take to the Other Side was this crummy gown, a pocket comb, and a box of Kleenex. You ought to see those dead pharaohs! The ancient Egyptians knew how to send a guy off in style. The pharaohs strut around in their jeweled crowns and gold breastplates, all their servants wait on them hand and foot, and even their damn cats purr in their laps!

"On the other hand," he continued, "this hospital treats its dying patients like an embarrassment, shunting them off in their rumpled gowns to Room 479. For my own amusement, I hummed 'Nearer My God to Thee' through my Kleenex and comb. Sounded real good, but nobody heard me."

Several ghosts attributed their demise to confusion over which bedside button to push. One old-timer groused, "There's a call button for the nurse, another button for the TV, and three buttons for adjusting your death bed. When I felt my last chest pain coming on, I panicked and started pushing buttons. First, I jackknifed myself in bed, then, instead of a nurse, I got Jerry Springer."

One thing all the ghosts seemed to agree on was that the actual death experience was totally pain-free and really quite comfortable. "A piece of cake!" said one see-through lady. "Didn't feel a thing. Just a sense of peace. After taking off in my new wings, I hovered over my bed for a few seconds, just long enough to flap good-bye forever to my walker and my HMO card."

17

The Rising of Cap Michaels

AT SEVENTY-TWO, CASPER ("CAP") MICHAELS was dying fast. The cat's cradle of ten lines of intravenous fluids dripping into him was barely prolonging his life. Dr. Welles, the hospital intensivist, told Cap's wife, daughter, and me, his long-time internist, that the patient had a 98 percent chance of dying within the next forty-eight hours. (The intensivist, a newly evolved super-specialist, is a dying patient's last hope.)

Despite this virtually hopeless prognosis, I emphasized to the family that once a heart attack victim has made it into an intensive-care bed at Alta Bates Hospital, there was always hope. At this, Dr. Welles raised his fierce eyebrows, indicating he thought that I, a lowly office internist, was not only out of my mind but also out of my depth. Nevertheless the family's reddened eyes lit up when I proffered them this morsel of hope.

An internist colleague once precisely described to me the meager role of the general internist in the modern hospital management of patients. "We can order laxatives," he said, "and talk to the family. And that's it."

The specialists, led by the omniscient intensivist, run the show at hospitals these days.

In the case of my ten-drip patient, laxatives were out of the question, but the family was eager for any word that was remotely optimistic.

The most powerful message a doctor can give a critically ill patient is hope—even if the patient is unconscious and this message must be delivered to the family.

Most doctors are confirmed optimists. But they must protect themselves from being accused of promising the sun, moon, and stars to a patient just before he's lowered into the earth. As a result they pull a long face in front of the patient and family. Then, if the patient survives, the doctors look all the more heroic. Provided the family has survived being worried to death.

I've never seen a patient more likely to die than my old friend and patient, Cap Michaels, a retired oil-company VP. He had suffered a silent infarct three days before being rushed to the ER. A silent infarct is a painless heart attack.

An insulin-dependent diabetic for most of his life, Cap had once told me he dealt with his diabetes as if it were a separate, full-time job. Cap checked his blood sugar three times a day, making the necessary pinpoint insulin adjustments. Like a California custom-car fanatic, he obsessively worked on his sleek body with daily aerobics and a strict diet, low in fat, moderate in carbohydrate, and moderate in protein.

At his country club, he played tennis more aggressively than his doctor ordered ("I take no prisoners on the tennis court"), but he seemed to thrive on competition. Almost all the men in his family had died of a stroke or heart attack in their forties and fifties. Having defeated his ancestors, he had deferred his own catastrophe till age seventy-two.

The reason he couldn't feel the usually crushing chest pain of a myocardial infarct was that his long-standing diabetes, no matter how well managed, had slowly injured the nerves that allowed him to perceive heart pain. He merely felt very weak for two days and wrote it off to "the flu." His adoring wife medicated him with echinacea and four grams of vitamin C daily.

When his severely damaged heart could no longer pump blood and quarts of his blood suddenly backed up into his lungs, his wife called 911. Even diabetic neuropathy can't mask the symptoms of suffocation.

By the time the paramedics arrived, Cap was unconscious and in massive heart failure. His blood pressure was unobtainable. Cardiogenic shock is one of the very few justifications for ambulances to speed to a hospital with drivers and sirens screaming through red lights.

The ER doctors and nurses were all over him the second he arrived. Already on 100 percent oxygen, he immediately became a four-drip patient: IV tubing began infusing drugs to increase his blood pressure, to control his suddenly chaotic heart rhythm, to lower his acutely elevated blood sugar, and to reduce the fluid overload in his lungs. Cap's initial cardiogram and blood tests indicated that 75 percent of his heart muscle had been taken out by his heart attack.

Set and match point, Death serving.

The forlorn hope in a situation like this is that some of the heart muscle damage might be reversible if we could buy time—if Cap's vital functions of breathing and pumping blood could be done for him. Dr. Welles, the intensivist, inserted a tube down Cap's trachea and hooked him up to an artificial ventilator. A cardiologist was summoned and deftly threaded a balloon pump into Cap's aorta to enhance the circulation that his destroyed heart could no longer maintain.

A half-hour after his arrival at the ER, Cap startled awake, began choking on his breathing tube, and tugging at his wrist restraints. Within two minutes he went from a four-drip to a ten-drip patient. Dr. Welles ordered the additional mainlining of a sedative, a narcotic, a muscle relaxant, a second antiarrhythmic, another drug to raise his extremely low blood pressure, and a plasmalike fluid to prevent shutdown of his kidneys. Cap fell into a deep sleep.

This was not exactly an occasion to enlist the patient's cooperation, as modern medical practice dictates. This was an occasion to transport the patient to Cloud 9 and pull out all stops in hopes of his not taking up permanent residence there. Over the next three days, $10,000 worth of medication dripped into him daily, his HMO be damned. Despite these extreme measures, his heart progressively failed.

On the fourth day his wife handed me a small round disk and asked, "Would you mind terribly taping this magnet to Cap's chest?" I had known his wife to be a true believer in alternative medicine, which so far had not undermined her own genetically excellent health. I politely declined her request, mumbling something about a magnet's interfering with the electrical monitoring of his heartbeat.

On the fifth day Cap suffered another heart attack. He went from drug-induced sleep into coma and his blood levels of cardiac enzymes went off the charts.

At this critical juncture something amazing happened. The hospital-based cardiac surgeon, Dr. Sidley, who had been pacing like a jackal on the periphery of this case, was called to the bedside by the intensivist. Dr. Welles urged Dr. Sidley to consider coronary bypass surgery on Cap as a last resort.

In my thirty-eight years as an internist I'd never heard anything like it. Shortly after admission the intensivist and a medical cardiologist had decided that Cap was too ill to survive coronary bypass surgery. Now that Cap was in even worse shape, *everyone* was recommending surgery and, of course, the cardiac surgeon agreed!

And they were right. After all medical efforts have failed, surgical revascularization is the patient's only chance to live. But we are talking state lottery odds.

The frantic wife and daughter eagerly agreed to this last-ditch measure. Unbelievably, Cap survived the operation and dramatically improved in the recovery room.

Deuce.

Over the next few days he was successfully weaned from the ventilator and the aortic balloon pump. Five days after surgery he had rallied sufficiently to complain of constipation. The ball, at last, was in my court. With a powerful forehand delivery, I scrawled an order for one ounce of milk of magnesia to be given at bedtime.

The next morning Cap, who had enjoyed a brilliant response to my laxative, drew me to his bedside and asked me to listen closely.

"I don't want to live," he whispered in my ear. "Why didn't you let me die?"

He was suffering from a massive postoperative depression compounded by weeks of confinement in the critical care unit. Serious psychiatric disorders are not uncommon after bypass surgery. Under constant fluorescent light, with three shifts of nurses and technicians turning and poking him every few minutes, a post-op cardiac patient loses all sense of time and ordinary reality.

His dramatic stay in the hospital had done wonders for his body but destroyed his spirit.

I tried to reassure Cap that his profound sadness was common and would pass with a little more time and the use of an antidepressant. But nothing seemed to cheer him up. The nurses had to force him to eat. A week later, when his cardiologist deemed him sufficiently recovered to be discharged home, everyone was overjoyed except Cap.

His family was sure he'd perk up once he got home.

On his discharge day his wife and daughter tied enormous red and blue helium balloons to his wheelchair in order to celebrate his miraculous recovery. Cap was not amused.

Slumped in his shiny, brand-new McReady wheelchair, Cap waited dolefully outside the hospital while his family drove up with their car.

What happened next might seem unbelievable, but you tend to find the unexpected commonplace if you've been in medicine long enough.

The morning of Cap's discharge day was sunny but very blustery. When the nurse who accompanied him picked up the heavy azalea plant Cap had insisted on carrying in his lap, he began to levitate. The 50-mph gusts, the six huge helium balloons, his custom-built, ultra-lightweight wheelchair, and Cap's current weight of eighty-two pounds conspired to create lift off.

He was last seen rising majestically above the hospital roof, and heading east. I can confirm that he was gazing heavenward with a beatific smile on his face.

After the nurse wrote out her incident report, there was only one thing left for me to do.

I talked to the family.

18

A Middle-Aged Doctor on the Middle Ages

WHO CAN DENY THAT WE OWE OUR EXISTENCE to the hardiness of our ancestors' sexual appetite?

In the Middle Ages the average life span was thirty-nine years, but that was apparently long enough for an abundance of slap and tickle with an extensive ripple effect. (See *The Canterbury Tales, The Decameron,* and the *Report of the Bureau of the Census,* U.S. Department of Commerce, 1990.)

Before we blame testosterone for wars, road rage, and the governor of Minnesota, let us acknowledge its historic role in the propagation of our species. Through the ages, testosterone, not alcohol, has been the primary chemical mediator of lust in both men and women. I submit that the Middle Ages were awash in testosterone, compared to the Modern Age, in which testosterone has slowed to a trickle.

In New York City, sperm counts, which are dependent on testosterone levels, have dropped 10 percent in the past twenty years. With each feeble orgasm, the male New Yorker produces only 150 million of the little fellows, 180 million tops.

If we extrapolate this trend back to fourteenth-century Florence, the average male Florentine would have sent forth enough spermatozoa per ejaculate (six billion plus) to populate the entire modern world as we know it—if he so desired. The intensity of the Florentine love ballad and the scarcity of empty tables at outdoor cafés everywhere in the civilized world indicate that, indeed, he so desired.

The amazing medieval libido survived not only the plague, small-pox, and leprosy, but also the ghastly treatments doctors inflicted on their victims. Bloodletting, purges, and herbal tonics laced with hemlock had unintended euthanasic effects, but not before they acted as aphrodisiacs.

Or so the evidence suggests.

It's a matter of record that during the Black Plague of the fourteenth century, licentious behavior was rampant. Along with fervent prayer and herbal tonics, sex was a major coping mechanism for those who had not yet been infected. A popular saying of the times, roughly translated, goes something like this:

"Offering a prayer, gathering herbs, and enjoying sex all bring men to their knees, but only sex brings smiles to their faces." —Anonymous

Prayer, herbs, and sex did nothing to stop the plague, which killed sixty million people in Europe, Africa, and Asia, or one-fourth of the world's population at the time.

Nowadays the very same plague is an easily treated medical curiosity seen occasionally after a cat bite. Two capsules a day of tetracycline, a cheap antibiotic, cures the plague in ten days. Tetracycline not only works better than sex, but unlike spermatozoa, comes in a childproof container. Trouble is, tetracycline did not become widely available until the early 1950s.

If this middle-aged doctor had practiced in the Middle Ages and had been able to prescribe tetracycline, I would have been branded "an alternative therapist" and burned at the stake.

The most sought-after medicine that apothecaries (forerunners of pharmacists) dispensed was called "treacle," which was considered virtually a cure-all. It was said to prevent internal swellings; cure fevers; unblock internal stoppages; alleviate heart problems, epilepsy, and palsy; get rid of blemishes; improve digestion; strengthen limbs; heal wounds; induce sleep; remedy snake bites; correct prolapsed uteruses; and cure the plague.

The formula for treacle stems from a recipe developed by the Greek physician, Galen, and was composed of more than sixty ingredients, including the roasted skin of vipers. Its major side effect was halitosis that could empty a ballroom. It took forty days to make and twelve years to mature.

And we complain about having to wait fifteen minutes for the pharmacist to fill our prescription!

Most medieval medicines were "simples" composed of herbal ingredients, which were taken raw or in teas. Except as placebos, they were worthless, but at least they didn't cause erectile dysfunction.

By contrast most of the drugs I prescribe in this enlightened age often cause erectile dysfunction, e.g., Zantac for heartburn, Naprosyn for arthritis, Tenormin for blood pressure, Zocor and Lipitor for high cholesterol, Valium and Xanax for anxiety, and Prozac and Paxil for depression. Thanks to these remarkable drugs, we are living longer with less heartburn and sadness, but at what cost!

When I think about it, Viagra is the only drug I prescribe that *doesn't* cause erectile dysfunction.

Actually, deep research indicates that Viagra was available in the lusty Middle Ages, but men found no use for it. Called "Vigaro" by the Italians since the early fifteenth century, it was first used by Florentine women as plant food to keep their gladiolas from drooping.

19

The Laughter of an Audience Is My Best Medicine

IN MY SUBSPECIALTY AS A STAND-UP COMEDIAN, from time to time I'm asked by physicians to speak on the healing power of humor at dinner meetings around the country. Before I can stand up, I'm required to sit down. For two hours I pretend to enjoy a microwaved hotel dinner with the medical strangers who were kind enough to ask me to address them. It's during the Cool Whip–topped dessert that I'm usually introduced and required to make my colleagues laugh.

When you combine stage fright with tough beef sirloin, a butter-infused baked potato, gloppy Caesar salad, jet lag, and a vintage Ohio red wine, what you end up with at the end of the meal is a patient in need of life support rather than a doctor prepared to amuse his hosts. The audience, similarly sated, usually has a hard time staying awake for dessert, let alone me. As often as not, it's a matter of the semicomatose addressing the somnolent.

My opening remarks are often drowned out by the clatter of dessert forks and the frequent sound of PLOOF as sleep-deprived physicians pitch forward, face-first, into their Cool Whip.

I was once flown to Cleveland to give a speech on humor in medicine to a group of family practitioners in a large Italian restaurant.

My host had failed to provide the two necessary ingredients for a talk of this kind: a microphone and a private banquet room.

My audience of physicians was seated at ten tables-for-eight in the center of the restaurant, surrounded by 120 Italian-Americans who were attending a wedding dinner for out-of-town guests. Dr. Jack Brewster, my medical host, a 250-pound former college halfback, introduced me in a booming voice that barely rose above the din of the Italian revelers.

Dr. Brewster's extravagant praise for my books fell on deaf ears as I stood up to zero applause. Resorting to sign language to convey his high regard for me, he good-naturedly clapped me on the back, almost sending me head first into a serving bowl of zabaglione on the adjacent table.

At top volume, my speaking voice was no match for what sounded like the full-throated chorus from a Puccini opera. The doctors couldn't hear a word I said despite rolling their menus into paper cones to serve as ear trumpets.

Successfully competing with my remarks, one of the Italian wedding guests sang an earsplitting love ballad in an off-tune tenor that was painfully strained during the high notes. I found myself shouting. Then, in one of those unpredictable moments of total silence sometimes experienced in a noisy restaurant, his song came to an end just as my joke climaxed. In the momentary silence that preceded the applause, I loudly delivered my punch line, "Give him an enema! It wouldn't hurt!"

Never in my life have I experienced such profound disapproval as that which was written on the highly expressive faces of 120 Italian-Americans, who glowered at me for the rest of the evening.

★ ✳ ★

The other week I spoke in San Francisco to a group of oncological gynecologists—surgeons who specialize in operating on women with cancer of the cervix, uterus, and ovaries. This grim subspecialty needed a little comic relief, I thought, when I accepted their invitation.

Instead of the usual forty minutes, it took me two harrowing hours to crawl with traffic over the Bay Bridge from Berkeley to San Francisco. In desperate need of a restorative, I arrived just as the cocktail hour ended and dinner was being served.

At least I had a microphone and a captive audience in a small, private banquet room.

The crowd consisted of about forty very pleasant cancer surgeons and their yawning wives, plus twelve Chinese physicians who had flown over from Beijing to learn the ropes of oncological gynecology. Everyone looked moderately jet-lagged and slightly inebriated.

As we shook hands before dinner, I learned that the Chinese doctors' command of spoken English was only slightly better than my language skills in Mandarin, which consisted largely of technical terms like "won ton" and "kung fu."

Separated only by language, I discovered that Chinese and Jewish physicians actually have much in common: We both grew up in a culture obsessed with family, education, and Chinese food. (On the other hand, we will never see eye-to-eye on the relative merits of ginseng and chicken soup.)

Now, my humor has a strong Jewish content, which I confidently predicted would elude the twelve Chinese guests who occupied a prominent table in the center of the room. Luckily Dr. Curtis Wang, my Chinese-American host, came to the rescue by translating my speech line-for-line into Mandarin. He did such a good job that his Chinese guests doubled over in laughter halfway through every one of my sentences.

"I've been in the solo practice of internal medicine for over thirty years," I said by way of self-introduction. Something was gained in translation when Dr. Wang's Mandarin version of this comment was followed by uproarious laughter from the visiting Chinese doctors. (Perhaps, I reflected later, the notion of a solo practitioner in a communist country was a risible concept to them.)

The beauty part was that their laughter was so infectious that the American doctors, who made up the bulk of the audience, became similarly convulsed. In past years, I had given this same speech dozens of times to scattered snickers and polite applause, but this was one of those magical evenings in show biz when everything comes up roses.

Remarkably the following line got my biggest laugh: "It took me more than two hours to cross the Bay Bridge." I learned later that my translator-host, Dr. Curtis Wang, is known as "the Oscar London of China."

Well, no wonder I knocked them dead.

20

The Kisswells' Fatal Attraction to Their Cat

IN THE PAST TWO YEARS I've become a wee bit concerned that the strident complaints of animal rights activists are impacting public opinion more than the muted pleas of human rights leaders. Hence, for your contemplation, the following scenario:

Marge and Elliott Kisswell had no children of their own, but no child could have given them greater joy than Deirdre, their blue-point Siamese cat. Deirdre slept on a down comforter in a small wooden replica of Bangkok's Temple of the Dawn. The comforter and temple were lovingly handcrafted by Marge and Elliott, respectively.

Deirdre dined on fresh calf's liver cut up into tiny cubes and served three times a day in an exquisite Lenox bowl of white china. No canned or packaged cat food ever touched Deirdre's raspy little tongue, you may be sure!

Deirdre's litter box was filled daily with fresh marble gravel flown in from Carrara, Italy.

To have her declawed and neutered, Marge and Elliott gladly wrote out a check for just under $12,000 to Deirdre's health care provider, Dr. Maurice Gingold, who was not your common flea-bitten vet but rather a felinologist with a degree from the Harvard School of Veterinary Gynecology in Lubbock, Texas.

In her fourteenth year, Deirdre developed an allergy. For months she sneezed constantly and often violently despite antihistamine pills and cortisone shots. Finally Dr. Anton Pemcoe, a veterinary allergist, performed an elaborate series of blood, skin, and environmental tests on Deirdre. Two weeks later when Dr. Pemcoe received the results from an immunological laboratory in Switzerland, he phoned Marge and Elliott Kisswell to come down to his office at once.

After the anxious Kisswells were seated in his consultation room, Dr. Pemcoe announced, "Let's cut to the chase: It seems Deirdre is allergic to Mrs. Kisswell. At first, we thought it might be the down comforter or dust mites. But, thanks to you, Mrs. Kisswell, a snippet of your locks, which you so graciously relinquished, clinched the diagnosis. Deirdre is severely and exclusively allergic to you."

Mrs. Kisswell paled visibly as her husband shot her an accusatory glance.

Dr. Pemcoe asked her, "Have you by any chance noticed that Deirdre's sneezing worsens as you approach her?"

"Yes," sobbed Marge Kisswell into her monogrammed hanky. "Deirdre hasn't let me come near her for months!"

"This is terrible," said Elliott Kisswell. "How do you cure such a thing, Doctor?"

"Let me first ask you a question," said Dr. Pemcoe, whose expressionless face did little to comfort Marge Kisswell. "Are you able to afford to put your wife up, say, in an apartment across town so that Deirdre is no longer directly exposed to the allergen, I mean, Mrs. Kisswell?"

"Out of the question," said Elliott. "I'm having to borrow money to pay your consultation fees! One of our Jaguars was repossessed just last week."

"In that case," concluded Dr. Pemcoe, "I'm afraid it will be necessary to put Mrs. Kisswell down."

"Excuse me?" said Marge Kisswell, with an incredulous smile on her face. "Surely you aren't proposing that. . . ."

"How much will THAT cost?" asked Elliott Kisswell.

For three years Elliott Kisswell and Deirdre, now completely cured, lived in contented proximity. Then one morning as Elliott approached Deirdre with her morning plate of liver, she began sneezing uncontrollably.

Elliott's suicide note indicated that he was leaving the bulk of his still-sizable estate to a trust that would provide 24/7 loving care for Deirdre in the Kisswell's matrimonial residence.

Deirdre, of course, couldn't have cared less about the considerable sacrifices made by her former owners as long as she continued to receive her three servings of fresh cubed liver each day in her white bowl of Lenox china.

At age thirty-two she died, with dignity, of a self-administered hairball.

21

The HMO *Insufferable* Hoists the Skull and Crossbones

WOULD YOU BE OFFENDED IF I RELATED the following observations about your grandmother to a colleague? "Except for a bit of worminess in her futtocks and the deplorable condition of her knees, she's in fairly good shape."

Actually those observations do not refer to your grandmother but rather to a frigate, specifically a late eighteenth-century English man-of-war. A futtock is a curved timber that forms a rib in the frame of a ship. The knees are wooden joints in the hull.

In recent months I've become obnoxiously nautical and seriously addicted to the seafaring novels of the late Patrick O'Brian. These riveting, beautifully written tales of love and war feature Captain Jack Aubrey of His Majesty's Royal Navy and his ship's surgeon, Dr. Stephen Maturin.

Mine is not a solitary addiction. Over twenty million copies of the twenty Aubrey–Maturin novels have been sold.

These books have transformed the way I perceive and practice medicine. I now clearly see myself as a latter-day Dr. Maturin, the brilliant, neurotic ship's surgeon of the HMS *Intrepid*, as it trades deadly broadsides with the HMO *Insufferable*.

In the eighteenth century, the Royal Navy took great pains to prevent scurvy by supplying vitamin C in the form of lime juice. (Thus the term, limeys, for British sailors.) To make sure the sailors swallowed their lime juice, which many found repellently sour, the ship's surgeon had it mixed with their daily ration of grog. Even this proto-margarita failed to prevent some cases of scurvy when a few of the sailors traded their grog for tobacco!

According to the protocol of the day, these rebellious, nicotine-addicted patients were forced to walk the plank—the original twelve-step program—if they refused to start sucking lime juice.

Constrained by current medical ethics, I tend to employ less drastic measures to prevent scurvy among my patients. Thanks to my heroic refusal to curb the widespread use of megadoses of vitamin C by Berkeley patients, I have yet to treat my first case of scurvy after thirty-eight years of practice! And you can put that in your pipe and smoke it.

In Dr. Maturin's day, the two most common remedies prescribed by a ship's surgeon on a man-of-war were amputation and bloodletting. And nobody did these procedures with more élan than Dr. Maturin. As a fanatic disciple of Patrick O'Brian, I've done my best to follow in Dr. Maturin's bloody footsteps.

Lately some of my patients have begun to grumble about my seemingly hasty recommendation for amputation of an infected limb when a dab of Neosporin ointment and a Band-Aid might appear do the trick. On a man-of-war, of course, you never questioned authority. *O tempora! O mores!*

Well, I've pulled back a bit on my limb-lopping policy, but so far no patient of mine has let out a peep over the liberal, periodic bloodletting that I prescribe under the guise of "getting lab tests." (Show me a patient who hasn't felt MUCH better as soon as the needle is withdrawn and I'll show you a masochist.)

Just about the worst thing that could happen to a man-of-war in heavy seas was to be pooped and broached to. In the nautical sense, to be pooped is to take a wave over the stern. In my practice the nearest I've seen to that definition of pooped occurred last year when a tired, elderly patient of mine suffered a wave over his stern when the plumbing suddenly backed up in my rest room.

Quick thinking on the part of my first mate (that would be my wife, who was working in the office at the time) saved this gentleman from broaching to, which means to veer broadside to the wind and waves, followed by sinking out of sight. My plumbing and locksmith bills were astronomical but, under the circumstances, worth every shilling.

Before I assumed the role of Dr. Maturin, I had been, like "Lucky Jack" Aubrey, the dashing captain of my office, which I commanded as if it were the HMS *Intrepid*. Like the gun deck of a man-of-war, my office was scrubbed and polished at dawn until it gleamed. When I arrived promptly at eight bells to inspect my first patient, I opened my closet to find the starched, immaculate white coat of a board-certified internist, standing at attention on its hanger.

As captain, my decision was final. When I ordered, "Take the estrogen!" there was no back talk. When I was piped aboard my ship, there was a Tobey jug of Sumatra coffee with a dram of half-and-half and a pinch of Equal waiting for me in my cabin, or there was hell to pay.

And then, to my astonishment, mutiny! Overnight, half my able-bodied patients switched their allegiance from the HMS *Intrepid* to the HMO *Insufferable*. I, the standard-bearer for Captain Aubrey, was replaced the next day by Captain Generic.

With my first mate, I was placed in a dinghy and ordered to shove off.

And not only mutiny, but the perfect storm! My beautiful ship that had navigated the tranquil seas of Fee-for-Service—its full sails in a westerly blossoming like a white rose—suddenly encountered the tsunami of Managed Care.

In less time than it takes to deny a request for a bone densitometry, the HMS *Intrepid* was pooped and broached to. It went down with all hands, while the pirates aboard the HMO *Insufferable* cheered.

Britannia no longer rules the waves while the HMO *Insufferable* waves the rules. God save the king! And American medicine!

Not even Patrick O'Brian could write his way out of this tragedy.

22

Managed Car

FOR THE PAST THIRTY-EIGHT YEARS I've practiced medicine in a small, stucco office building on Webster Street in Berkeley. Like Hobbes's definition of primitive life, Webster Street is "nasty, brutish, and short." It runs down the middle of a medical ghetto where patients and doctors suffer a common misery known as managed care.

I drive a once elegant, now decrepit, '86 Lincoln Town Car originally purchased in the last flush of fee-for-service medicine.

At 10:00 A.M., a half-hour late for my first appointment, I turn onto Webster, brake for a pregnant surgeon crossing the street, then creep behind cars driven by eye-patched seniors and overdosed melancholics. Five minutes and a hundred feet later, before I can begin my left turn into the garage below my building, I must slam on my brakes again.

A twenty-year-old taxi is parked across the driveway. Like an unruffled obstetrician performing a breech delivery, the third-world cabby slowly extracts an elderly passenger from the backseat, feet first, along with her walker.

As the taxi meter ticks patiently away, I pound my steering wheel and shout a non-Hippocratric oath behind the closed windows of my Lincoln.

A year ago we tenants urged the owners of the building to bring order to the chaotic parking lot. In response they licensed the parking operation to a newly arrived immigrant from India. In order to avoid paying him a salary, the landlords declared him an independent contractor, with a cut of the parking fees going to the owners. Only in America.

The whole morning scenario underwent a dramatic change. Now as my car approaches, Mr. Sundar Patel, the nimble seventy-two-year-old garage attendant, charges up the driveway, shouting at an obstructing cab driver to hurry up. With a flick of his wrist, Mr. Patel snaps open a patient's walker, props her up in it, then hustles the cabbie back into his impaired vehicle.

As the taxi departs with an unmuffled roar, Mr. Patel disappears in a blue cloud of exhaust fumes. Materializing at the bottom of the driveway, he signals me to ease my creaky, multidinged Town Car down the steeply graded ramp into the garage. With tight arm movements and controlled panic in his eyes, he resembles a landing officer on an aircraft carrier, waving in the wounded pilot of a shot-up F14.

In his anxiety to serve me, Mr. Patel, a bronze-skinned, silver-haired gentleman, reveals more than a vestige of his early years in colonial Bombay under the British Raj. Attired in sharply creased, polyester slacks, a previously owned but well-maintained sports jacket and floppy sandals, he is the frequently disputed master of his domain: the pitiful eighteen-car garage below our building.

Eleven of the places are reserved for the building's tenants and their staff. This leaves just seven hotly contested spaces for the dozens of patients who visit the building daily. Among Mr. Patel's duties, for which I tip him ten bucks each month, is keeping renegade patients out of my hallowed, reserved parking space, which boasts strata of fossil-fuel deposits dating back more than three decades.

In one corner of the garage Mr. Patel has set up a bridge chair and an old wicker table on which rests an antique TV set, a third-hand boom box, an incense burner, and a plastic bud vase containing a red silk rose. On the utility door behind him he's taped colorful posters of Hindu deities, the muscular gods heavily mustached, the bosomy goddesses deeply indented at the waist.

In his corner of this foreign field that is forever India, his sickly greenish TV screen is his jewel in the crown. To judge from his laughter, Mr. Patel's favorite program is the frightfully vulgar British sitcom, *Are You Being Served?*

Since Mr. Patel's contract with the building allows him to charge only a dollar an hour for each of the few available parking places, I worried at first about how he could make a living. I didn't know then of his extraordinary talent for applied geometry.

In addition to the diagonal parking spaces against its side and back walls, the garage has a narrow central area in which cars can maneuver while heading in to park or backing out to escape. It's within this nondescript area, roughly sixty by twenty feet, that this mathematically gifted Indian, a latter-day Ramanujan, has worked out his amazing theories of triple parking in series.

When a patient arrives, Mr. Patel stops the car at the foot of the ramp and confiscates the ignition key and a one-dollar advance payment. In his early attempts at garage parking, Mr. Patel's limited, perhaps nonexistent, knowledge of how to operate a motor vehicle was all too apparent.

Before he accidentally discovered the function of the clutch pedal on a new Porsche, he had frequently been pulled bodily from behind the steering wheels of lurching cars by outraged owners, some of whom needed cardiograms when they finally saw their doctors.

This break-in period was blessedly brief, and within weeks Mr. Patel was parking cars with the aplomb and precision of a teenage parking valet at a San Francisco restaurant.

He soon learned the rhythms of the various doctors in the building so he could judge how long it would take for a car to be reclaimed by a visiting patient. My patients, for example, took forever, what with waiting an eternity to see me, then paying me back with Homeric recitations of their obscure symptoms.

Mr. Patel would park my patients in the static inner tier of his grand design. By contrast, visits by patients of Dr. Austin Braddock, the general surgeon, were brief affairs—a dressing change, a pat on the back, and out the door. Their cars were placed in the more fluid, outer perimeter.

The Patel method worked like a charm. All day, cars were triple-parked down the center of the garage. His pockets bulged with one-dollar bills. Mr. Patel had made it in America.

I came to enjoy the south Asian ambience he brought to our little garage in Berkeley. As I walked toward the elevator after parking, the sinuous whine of the sitar on Mr. Patel's boom box seemed to lighten my limbs, while the exotic aroma of his incense filled my head. Blissfully I entered the elevator and was borne aloft to my office on a rising cloud of Bombay muzak admixed with Fumes of Exhilaration.

Mr. Patel's caste system of judging doctors was based on the expense of their cars. With his new Mercedes 560 SEL, Dr. Braddock was the Brahmin while I, the less than proud owner of an '86 Lincoln, was the untouchable (except for the ten bucks he touched me for each month).

It was on a Wednesday in September that Mr. Patel's parking enterprise achieved critical mass, followed abruptly by Armageddon. I saw the whole thing. The garage that day was jammed with unusually expensive cars. It was inside this compact version of a *concours d'élégance* that Mr. Patel reinvented the demolition derby. It began with the appearance of a red-and-rust 1963 Ford pickup truck, driven by a twenty-year-old indigent roofer.

Until then Mr. Patel's on-the-job training had consisted of parking the well-maintained, relatively new automobiles of the patients. He was ill-prepared to bring off one of his signature back-and-fill maneuvers behind the wheel of a thirty-three-year-old Ford pickup with faulty brakes. After he shifted into reverse, the first inkling that he'd overestimated this vehicle's braking power was a loud crunching sound. The back of the truck had plowed into the left front fender of a beige '98 Jaguar Vanden Plas.

Shifting noisily into first, Mr. Patel extricated truck from Jaguar. After lurching ten feet forward, he slammed on the brakes only to look on helplessly as the front of the truck crushed the black, deeply polished trunk of a BMW 730i. His delicately shaped hands still gripping the wheel of the pickup, Mr. Patel sat pale and dazed.

Dr. Nigel Sneed-Jones, one of the building's landlords, shot out of his ground floor office at the first sound of metal on metal. He began screaming imprecations at Mr. Patel that set back Anglo-Indian relations one hundred years.

I confess to a slight frisson of schadenfreude when I learned that Dr. Sneed-Jones and his partners, the "deep pockets" in the case, had been successfully sued by the owners of the damaged cars.

Overnight Mr. Patel and his little corner of India disappeared from the garage. Sadly I assumed I'd never again levitate on a cloud of music and incense before confronting the faceless monster of managed care that lay in wait behind my office door.

One morning, a month after Armageddon, I found Mr. Patel—or was it his wraith?—standing at the entrance of the garage. Instead of his tweed sports jacket, he wore a long, starched white coat that sported a logo over its breast pocket, "Webster St. Parking, Inc." When he saw me, he pressed his palms together and bowed slightly at the waist, his once animated face a blank.

Behind him the formerly bustling garage was quiet as a mausoleum, each car laid out neatly in its assigned stall. Mr. Patel's elaborate triple parking configurations had vanished along with his Indian artifacts. Now the only aroma in the garage was that of exhaust fumes and despair, the only sound that of two palms pressing.

Like me Mr. Patel was now a low-salaried servant of a soulless corporation—in his case, the building's owners.

He recently told me he's looking around for another kind of business, where he can earn more for his skills and hard work. Nodding sympathetically I opened the trunk of my Lincoln to reveal an extensive display of Amway products. (The new cars don't have nearly the trunk capacity of an '86 Town Car.)

"Mr. Patel," I asked, "can I perhaps interest you in a five-pound box of detergent?"

23

Don't Diet, Medicate!

AFTER THIRTY-EIGHT YEARS of watching lovely people sicken and die from the ravages of obesity and inactivity, I have no illusions that my exhortations to diet and exercise will ever be heeded.

If vanity doesn't inspire you to eat less and exercise more, nothing will, including the fear of dying young. For those whose genetics and *joie de vivre* are keeping them roly-poly and laid-back, there's still hope for a long and healthy life.

Medication. Drugs not to lose weight, but to treat the consequences of obesity. With what is now available to lower high levels of cholesterol, blood sugar, and blood pressure, we may be able to have our cake and eat almost all of it too. Heresy is my middle name.

As you may have heard, the five-year cure rate for lung cancer is 5 percent, versus 2 percent for obesity—which, for example, would amount to losing twenty-five pounds and KEEPING IT OFF for five years. In other words, you're more than twice as likely to be cured of lung cancer than of obesity.

The 2 percent who manage this rare feat, transform themselves from overweight, lovely people into the biggest bores on the planet. But thin. Far into their nursing home years, they wheel swiftly up and down the corridors searching for someone to be amazed at how little they had for breakfast.

Small wonder each year spawns another best-seller on how to lose weight. A million copies of *The Amazing Lettuce Diet* are sold and twenty-five million pounds of weight are lost. The next year the readers gain thirty million pounds and the next hundred thousand copies of the book, like so much lettuce, are shredded by the publisher. Come to think of it, a shredded book of 225 pages contains only 580 calories of starch, which suggests next year's best-seller, *Eat My Words*.

I've actually met a best-selling "nutritionist" whose handsome royalties five years ago led to his gaining forty-five pounds from sitting at the best tables in the finest restaurants in the world. Then his trophy wife sued him for divorce. Now he's just another starving writer whose worst fate is that he will live skinny and unpublished for the next forty years.

His only consolation is that his affluent ex-trophy now weighs 212 pounds. (Ask any doctor what the difference is between "trophy" and "hypertrophy.")

We've all heard the expression "You can't be thin enough or rich enough." Well, take it from me, who's neither, it's much easier to be rich enough than thin enough—unless you were born with a silver spoon in your mouth (detected by ultrasound in the second trimester) from parents who are genetically thin.

It's also much easier to exercise than diet, but given the cost of a personal trainer, you'll end up thin enough but not rich enough. If you eschew personal trainers and opt for jogging, you can be thin enough and rich enough into your fifties. Then your knees will give out and you'll grow fat in your rocking chair—rich enough but not thin enough. A year later you'll be neither, when your knees are replaced by prostheses not covered by your HMO.

No nutritional scientist will dispute the fact that semistarvation and lap swimming are marvelous for your health, as opposed, say, to gluttony and lap dancing.

Many of these scientists die young from sitting inert on their laboratory stools for years on end, observing obese, lazy mice clutch their fat little chests and die.

Trouble is, diets emphatically don't work. Their most vociferous advocates remind me of Oscar Wilde's definition of fox hunters: the unspeakable in pursuit of the inedible. And appetite suppressants make you so nervous, you'll lose friends and pounds for a few months until the pounds return, but not your friends. Drugs that reduce absorption of fat cause staining of your underwear. Rich enough and thin enough for what? Designer diapers?

Until that magic day when an effective diet pill is invented with a stainless reputation, we can use other drugs that will keep us alive and well and portly into our eighties. Vegans and marathon runners: read no further!

I never met a high LDL cholesterol I couldn't zap with a "statin" like Lipitor, Zocor, or Pravachol, no matter how fat the patient. Statins not only lower your cholesterol but prevent sudden death. They stabilize your coronary plaques, preventing their rupture. Why would you risk blowing out a coronary plaque during a jog? So you can die with your Adidas on?

Same goes for an elevated fasting blood sugar in an overweight adult, a condition known as diabetes II. I have a choice of five unrelated drugs that will drive down that sugar to normal, damn the corpulence.

As for hypertension, "the silent killer," you can quietly bump it off with an ACE-inhibitor like Zestril, a beta-blocker like Norvasc, a mild diuretic like HCTZ, or sometimes all three taken together. It's shameful how infrequently American doctors treat hypertension; more than half their patients are left to their own deadly devices.

Besides, what's wrong with being overweight like almost half the nation? At the current rate, it will be un-American to be thin in the new millennium.

This is the dirty secret of modern medicine: You can remain fat and lazy, but if you take the right medication and don't smoke, you can live WELL into your eighties. Unlike Winston Churchill, who chose Scotch and cigars as his medications and lived poorly into his nineties.

And this is the dirty secret of the heavyset man (which I alluded to in essay number 4): His blood levels of bioavailable testosterone are higher—as are his libido and erectile function—than if he were at "normal weight." Viagra is for the skinny geezer.

Another advantage of being chubby late in life: You will look younger in your face and limbs than your gaunt, wrinkled peers. They will have flatter abdomens that on close inspection look like a bird's-eye view of mud flats during a drought, but *your* belly will be as round and smooth as a polished Macintosh apple—the kind, unlike my iMac, with the sap inside.

Admittedly hypercholesterolemia, diabetes, and hypertension are *much* better treated with a lifetime of diet and exercise. Your doctor will then bless you with the famous left-handed compliment: "You are disgustingly healthy."

If you can't hack these lifestyle changes, you can still enjoy the same 40 percent reduction in the incidence of premature disease and death. Just find an old chunk-style doctor like me who'll convince you that your unhealthy numbers are pushovers for a few miracle pills you can take once or twice a day. Six months later, your doctor will take your pudgy hand in his and declare, "You are miraculously healthy."

Or, if you refuse to take his pills, announce, "I don't feel a pulse." I, for one, would rather sit back with my plaque, munching Pravachol and Pringles while peering over my paunch at *Ally McBeal*.

24

Two Ladies from Martinez

FOR AN INTERNIST, MAKING A DIAGNOSIS of an exceedingly rare and eminently curable disorder is the medical equivalent of a grand slam homer. Old-timer that I am, I must go back several decades to recount the day I hit two consecutive bases-loaded, round-trippers.

Maria and Gina, as I will call them, were two Italian-American ladies in their early forties who lived in the community of Martinez, California, about twenty miles north of Berkeley. Newly arrived in America from a small town in southern Italy, they were first cousins.

At the insistence of another cousin, Gabriella, who had been my steadfast patient for five years, Maria and Gina were driven to my doorstep one Monday morning twenty-five years ago. (Italian-American patients are among my most loyal and grateful patients— when they aren't being my severest critics.)

The two cousins, Maria and Gina, needed Gabriella as their translator and, more important, as their motivator to see me. Gabriella introduced me to the two shy ladies who were dressed in their Old World Sunday best. Maria was plain and stout. Gina was beautiful and curvaceous. Both wore deep vertical frown lines on their foreheads and dark circles under their bloodshot eyes.

Their American cousin, Gabriella, wearing blue jeans and a white blouse, told me that the two immigrants were driving her crazy. Day and night, since their arrival two months ago, they complained of shortness of breath, severe tiredness, depression, and insomnia.

At first Gabriella blamed her cousins' complaints on jet lag, but after a month, she was sure their escalating problems had something to do with their husbands, "Federico" and "Pasquale." These two fiery, hardworking carpenters had been enjoying the blessings of the legendary American freedom for a year before they could afford to bring over their wives and six kids (three boys for each family).

According to Gabriella, the two newly united families spent a lot of time shouting epithets and vigorously slamming doors (which would have easily shattered but for the superior workmanship of Federico and Pasquale).

The two miserable cousins, newly washed up on our shores by a flood tide of tears, confessed to Gabriella that they were too sick and tired to cook and take care of the kids, let alone perform any of the other expected wifely duties. Both complained mostly of fatigue and shortness of breath on the slightest exertion. Enter Dr. London.

When I opened the door of the exam room to see Maria, the plainer of the two sisters, I was taken aback to find her sitting unselfconsciously nude on my exam table. She was covered only by a Kleenex, which she held to her right eye. When I suggested to Gabriella that Maria might be more comfortable and less chilled in one of my lovely paper gowns, Gabriella explained that this was the way doctors in the old country preferred to examine their patients. "Well, when in Rome . . ." I said to myself, taking Maria's blood pressure.

Except for being overweight, Maria appeared completely normal until I got to her heart. It sounded fine while she sat up—no sign of enlargement, rhythm disturbance, or murmurs. I then instructed her through Gabriella to lie down on her left side on the examining table.

As I said, I was young in those days, not too removed from the rigorous discipline of my medical training. Besides, I had the luxury of time in a not-yet-overcrowded practice. Thanks to fanatic drilling by my medical school instructor in cardiology, I dutifully had my patients lie down on their left side during my examination of their hearts.

What I was listening for in that position was the murmur of the deadly heart-valve disease known as mitral stenosis—a distinctive rumble before the first heart sound. I had frequently read about it but had never heard it. Not in medical school, internship, residency, nor private practice. But I kept listening.

Bent over Maria's body, I placed the bell of my stethoscope over the apex of her heart, fully expecting to hear the "lub-dup" of a normal heart. Instead I heard something that gave me chills and still does when I think about it. It was a low-pitched sound, like distant thunder, that inserted itself in the interval between the "dup" of the second heart sound and the "lub" of the next, first heart sound.

This was the famous rumbling diastolic murmur of the rare, often fatal, but potentially curable disease known as mitral stenosis. Listening more carefully, I heard a high-pitched third heart sound as well, known as "the opening snap."

The opening snap was the crack of my bat hitting the baseball. The loud, crescendo rumble that followed was the roar of the crowd as the ball sailed over the center field bleachers. A grand slam, and it was only Monday morning!

The patient and her cousin visibly paled when they saw the astonished look on my face. I explained as best I could to Gabriella that there was a marked narrowing of the mitral valve between the left upper chamber (atrium) of Maria's heart and the left lower chamber (ventricle). This narrowing impaired her general circulation and accounted for her fatigue and shortness of breath. Through Gabriella, I asked Maria if she had had frequent sore throats as a child. Maria nodded.

The life-threatening condition of mitral stenosis is the result of inflammation and scarring of the mitral valve consequent to repeated, untreated strep infections. Since the advent of penicillin, which had never met a strep throat it couldn't cure, mitral stenosis was becoming increasingly uncommon in the United States.

By contrast Maria grew up in abject poverty in an Italy newly ravaged by World War II. Penicillin was unavailable in her childhood. I was able to tell Maria and Gabriella that the treatment of mitral stenosis was often spectacularly successful but required a relatively simple and very safe heart operation. I gave each of them a Valium tablet.

Next.

Cousin Gina, whom Gabriella had unnecessarily described as the town beauty, was already undressed and ready to be examined in the next room. Gabriella, sworn to secrecy for the time being about Maria, walked through the door with me. With the translator's help, I elicited the same history of fatigue and shortness of breath from Gina. I examined the patient's head, eyes, ears, nose, throat, and lungs first, as I was taught, before addressing her heart.

To my total surprise and, I confess, disappointment, Gina's heart sounded completely normal both in the seated position and in the "left lateral decubitus" position. Undeterred, I asked Gina to hop on one foot twenty-five times on the floor, then climb back on the table and lie down on her left side again.

Under less clinical circumstances, the sight of this lovely unclad woman, rhythmically hopping on one slender foot would have riveted my male attention. Under the circumstances I couldn't wait for the twenty-fifth hop so I could listen again to her exercise-stimulated heart.

As she rearranged herself, flushed and breathless, in the left lateral position, I placed the bell of my stethoscope with a trembling hand against the apex of her heart. Her heart rate had sped up to 130 beats per minute, making it difficult to listen to diagnostically. I had to wait a minute until it slowed to about 100 beats.

The opening snap and the diastolic rumble, brought out of hiding by the enforced exertion, were waiting for me.

I swung, connected, and the ball sailed in a high arc over the left field fence. I had hit my first and second grand slam home runs, consecutively, with the help of two ladies from Martinez, California—the hometown, incidentally, of Joe DiMaggio.

In those halcyon days before managed care, I proudly sent the two anxious patients off to a renowned cardiac surgeon at the University of California Hospital in San Francisco, without a hassle. In less than thirty minutes for each procedure, he successfully pried open the partially fused, fibrotic cusps of their mitral valves in a splendid operation known as a mitral valve commissurotomy.

Their circulation dramatically restored, Maria and Gina at last breathed freely, as I did, when they returned home to their vastly relieved and grateful families.

Space does not permit a catalog of the mouth-watering Italian delicacies that have made their way from Martinez to my office in Berkeley over the ensuing years.

Since the day of my consecutive grand slams twenty-five years ago, I've not heard one other heart afflicted with mitral stenosis.

But I have no regrets. There's nothing more indelible than the happy memories of old ballplayers and internists.

25

God Bless Firefighters

I LIKE POLICE OFFICERS, BUT I LOVE FIREFIGHTERS. I suppose I would love police officers too, but vivid memories of bright red, yellow, and blue lights blinking in my rearview mirror dull my passion. My being a doctor used to excuse me from any number of speeding tickets. I simply flashed my caduceus like a Christian holding a vampire at bay with a crucifix.

But the new generation of cops has no respect for the medical profession. They write up my ticket as if I were a run-of-the-mill scofflaw rather than a health-care professional scofflaw.

Firefighters, on the other hand, are totally admirable and lovable, with the exception of a few racists and sexists who should be, as they say in the trade, fired. For the most part, I love those guys and gals in the big red trucks. You don't hear a nickname like "cops" applied to firefighters. "Squirts?" Never!

Like doctors they're in the business of saving lives. Unlike doctors they risk their lives saving yours. And will sometimes die trying to preserve your property.

I recently talked with Brad, a firefighter from a small town in Northern California. Brad unequivocally states that his profession is the most gratifying on earth. "After a fire we have instant feedback.

When we're successful the family treats us like gods. Even if we *almost* save a life, or a burning home, the survivors are right there to tell us how grateful they are for our trying as hard as we did."

This contrasts to my profession: When I *almost* save a life, I also get instant feedback. From a law office.

✴ ✳ ✴

Today I had to call our local fire department to pick up a 220-pound patient who had fallen to the floor of my back examining room. He's a retired stockbroker in his late sixties who was seeing me for a routine follow-up visit.

Six months ago he suffered a massive right-brain stroke, leaving his speech intact but his left arm and leg paralyzed. Rather than ask me to make a house call, the patient had kindly insisted on coming to my office. This involved calling an "ambu-cab," which transported him, strapped to his wheelchair. His exhausted wife came along for the ride. (A severe stroke, like Alzheimer's, takes the whole family down with the patient.)

He and his wife, whom I will call Mr. and Mrs. Henderson, had been ushered into my relatively spacious back examining room by Melodie, my promising new office manager. Melodie promised, "Doctor London will be with you in just a few minutes." Well, as I said, she's new. But lovely. In my office, the only patients who wait "just a few minutes" are the ones who walk out because I didn't see them instantly.

While the Hendersons waited patiently, I was in Room Two, concluding my famous "depression is a biochemical disorder" speech to a very sad young man. Suddenly I heard that most off-putting of sounds in a doctor's office: a dull, heavy thud.

Melodie was right after all; I saw Mr. Henderson on time, leaving the depressed patient in midprotest over my prescription for Zoloft.

Mr. Henderson lay flat on his back, after suddenly sliding to the floor from his wheelchair. This mishap occurred when his frictionless cotton sweatpants slid over the balding lamb's wool on the seat of his wheelchair. Slouched in the chair, his heavy body, unimpeded by his lax seat belt, had abruptly surrendered to gravity.

Mr. Henderson's cherubic face lit up with an apologetic smile. "Sorry to drop in on you like this," he said. He denied he was in any pain. In fact he wasn't even aware that his left side was paralyzed. This common neurologic consequence of a stroke is called *la belle indifférence.*

Although he seemed quite content to rest on the floor, Melodie and I instinctively grabbed each of his shoulders and hoped his good right leg could work with us to lift him back into the chair.

"It's no use," Mrs. Henderson said. "He's a dead weight. Our whole family was in back braces until we learned to call the fire department." Melodie and I released our grip and Mr. Henderson subsided onto the carpet.

The response time of the fire department was under two minutes. Larger than life, two young heroes and one heroine marched through the door of my office and into the back room. They recognized me.

These same firefighters had been frequently summoned during the past three years to rush my semiconscious patient, "Millicent Ashford," to Alta Bates, our local hospital. Millicent was the matriarch of a large, distinguished family, most of whom were my patients. They invited my wife and me to all their family functions, from christenings to funerals.

In one of our fleeting episodes of darkest cynicism, my wife and I figured that the illustrious Ashfords had befriended us largely to assure that a doctor (that would be me) was on hand when Millicent hit the floor with one of her spells. Her type of spell is called *vaso-vagal syncope*—a dead faint followed by spontaneous resurrection, without resuscitation.

I soon learned to stuff a stethoscope next to my cellular phone in the side pocket of my navy blue blazer whenever we were invited to an Ashford event. Millicent seemed to choose the most lovely moment of each family event to roll her eyes back and drop her fashionably thin body noiselessly to the floor.

Until the fire department paramedics responded to my 911 call, I played my ceremonial role of attentive doctor. I bent over the unconscious but quietly breathing form of the prostrate Millicent, listening to her heart.

Crashing the party, three buff firefighters scooped her up and packed her off to the hospital. She invariably recovered on being wheeled into the emergency room. (Frankly I think she had a thing for firemen.)

Last January, as the minister was about to pronounce the Ashfords' youngest daughter and her groom "man and wife," Millicent struck again: Before four hundred guests in the lavishly decorated ballroom of the Claremont Hotel and Resort, Millicent swooned into the carpeted aisle, taking a 100-foot row of white orchids and a Jewish internist—that would be me—with her.

By the time Millicent hit the deck at the stately funeral of her renowned brother a week later, the paramedics and I were on a first-name basis.

So you can understand why the firefighters, when they appeared at my office to help levitate Mr. Henderson, all called out, "Hi, Oscar!"

"Hi, Ted. Hi, Neal. Hi, Sheryl," I replied.

Now, summoning an ambulance to a doctor's office is like hauling coals to Newcastle, but in this case I had to take my lumps. In two shakes of the lamb's wool tail, they had a beaming Mr. Henderson sitting upright and firmly secured. He winked flirtatiously at Sheryl, who winked back.

As the firefighters headed out, they stopped abruptly at Exam Room Two and looked down at the carpet. Through the open door protruded a tiny pair of Ferragamos pointed upwards. Millicent Ashford had struck again!

Like Olivier in the last act of *Hamlet,* her motionless body was borne aloft on a litter and carried, with great panache, by uniformed attendants down the hallway. Exit left.

God, I love firefighters!

26

How to Cut Your Doctor's Bill in Half

SOMETIMES THE BEST WAY TO HEAL IS TO WAIT. But these days when we're speeding through life, who has time to take time?

Herewith, cautionary tales of three conditions—back pain, sinusitis, and bronchitis—and some advice on how you can magically cure yourself of each of them.

Back Pain: Father Time Is on Your Side

Almost all back pains get well on their own, but you could die waiting for that to happen.

My job as an internist is to convince the patient with back pain to lie down at home rather than in the office of a chiropractor or physical therapist.

Severe back pain is mostly due to lumbar ligament sprain or a pinched sciatic nerve.

In my long experience with long-suffering back patients, I've learned that whoever has his or her hand on the patient's back when the sprain or pinched nerve decides to go away gets credit for the cure.

This is how chiropractors and physical therapists get reputations for being miracle workers. All they've done is keep the patient under their thumb until, despite them, the back pain disappears.

In a recent study published in the *New England Journal of Medicine,* researchers found that chiropractors and physical therapists produced equal but marginal benefit for acute back pain. Patients whose treatment consisted only in reading a booklet on back pain fared almost as well.

I strongly believe that passage of time and avoidance of improper lifting are the best treatments for back pain. Most patients lack the time and patience for this approach.

When it comes to back pain, this Jewish internist bows to the Christian Scientist, but not too low, lest I sprain my back. At most I'm a minimal interventionist.

At first I prescribe one day of bed rest and ice packs. Then a short course of codeine-class medication if needed, followed by Celebrex and hot baths.

Usually after four to eight weeks the patient wakes up one morning cured.

Remember, the last person to have his or her hand on the patient's back at the end gets credit for the cure. With my hands-off approach patients can pat themselves on the back when it's over and take the credit for the cure.

Sinusitis: "But the TV Ads Say You Should Give Me This Antibiotic"

Sinusitis is another grinder of an illness with its own agenda. Ninety percent of cases are viral or allergic, or a combination of both. Only 10 percent are bacterial. But you can bet your HMO's bottom dollar that if you see a doctor for sinusitis, you will not leave the office without a prescription for an antibiotic. Mea culpa.

After several weeks of pain and snuffling, these patients come to me and demand the latest antibiotic they saw advertised on TV. They want Zithromax! Since it's very difficult to rule out a bacterial cause for sinusitis, I usually give in and prescribe an antibiotic.

As a protest against TV ads for prescription drugs, I use Biaxin instead of Zithromax.

If the patient gets much better within three days, the antibiotic was the correct choice. If, as more often happens, they're still snuffling after two more weeks, the antibiotic at best served as a placebo and at worst as a stimulus to the formation of resistant bacteria.

Unless you have fever and severe facial pain, you might want to treat your sinusitis on your own by eating well, resting well, and taking over-the-counter decongestants, plus ibuprofen for pain. Trust me, you'll get well within three weeks.

If not, throw in the towel or Kleenex and see your doctor, who might want to make your HMO squirm by ordering sinus X rays before prescribing the ritual antibiotic.

Bronchitis: Why Not Try the Home Spa Treatment?

Another illness that tends to get better on its own is acute bronchitis (almost always viral), which can give you four to six weeks of hacking before saying "Uncle."

If you have chills and fever, or need understandable assurance and an unnecessary antibiotic, see your doctor before the six-week mark.

Meanwhile be your own internist with nonprescription cough syrup, a high-protein diet, hot sugary tea, and salty broth.

You can convert your bathroom into a spa by filling it with steam from super-hot shower water. Then sit down and breathe the decongesting vapors and visualize Tahiti. This costs you less than a buck in hot-water bills and not more than $800 if your wallpaper peels off.

Above all keep out of health-food stores—the healthier-than-thou customers will resent your nonstop coughing, and you'll waste a small fortune on echinacea and ginseng.

Be your own internist for your cough rather than your own quack for your hack.

If you're still coughing after three weeks, see your doctor for a chest X ray and possibly an antibiotic. Your prolonged coughing may be due to a touch of asthma you never knew you had and which your doctor can effectively treat.

Even after your immune system has killed off the virus that caused your bronchitis, you can still cough for six or more weeks due to "irritative bronchitis." This means the lining of your bronchial tree remains red and angry long after the virus has been killed.

At the six-week mark your bronchial tubes are about to undergo a spontaneous cure. It's often at this point that, out of desperation, you consult your herbalist or homeopath who will get credit for the cure that only your patience and common sense have brought about.

If you're about to get well anyway, at least see your internist. Nowadays we need all the respect we can get.

27

Wince, Ballerina, Wince

BALLET DANCERS CLASSICALLY SUFFER great physical and mental stress. So do ballet audiences. During a recent performance of the San Francisco Ballet, my wife and I were shocked to see a rather graphic rape scene being danced on the stage. We had emphatically stipulated at the box office that we wanted tickets for no more than one rape this season and, suddenly, we're seeing our third!

For a physician, modern and classical ballet offer little relief from a bad day in the ER—stabbings, poisonings, drownings, strangulations, gunshot wounds, sexual assault, beatings, and acute psychotic breaks. So much for Act I, Scene I.

Between these emergencies I tend to fall asleep in my front-row seat. From time to time I'm startled awake by the percussion section in the pit just below me. I look up to see a young woman in a miniskirt being stabbed by a man wearing frontally bulging leotards.

And, a few minutes later, what does the audience do to the girl and the brute who has just stabbed her? They appropriately deliver flowers to the victim, then give her killer a standing ovation! *Ars longa, vita brevis.*

From a medical standpoint, ballet dancers appear to have solved the great health challenges of diet and exercise. On closer inspection the ballerinas often look like they've been on purgatives and the male dancers on steroids. Then the music starts and they become airborne gods and goddesses.

Ballet is that rarest of aesthetic phenomena: a female-centered art form. In the metaphor of football, the ballerina is the quarterback and the male dancer, the wide receiver. Do these ballerinas slim down excessively in order to lighten the load for their male partners? I don't think so.

Who decreed that the beautiful women who are drawn to a career in ballet must efface their female contours in order to succeed? Balanchine? (Sounds like Ball and Chain.) I say bring the bosom and the buttocks back to ballet! The men can handle it, I'm sure.

Arguably ballet requires more physical exertion and emotional control than any other art form. And the toll on the dancers' bodies and minds indicates to me that ballet is not only an art form but also a disease.

Among ballerinas, excesses of weight loss and exercise lead to amenorrhea, early osteoporosis, stress fractures, and chronic fatigue syndrome. At about age thirty-five, when gravity begins to reclaim these soaring swans, there's not much left of them besides skin, bones, and bunions. Almost all retire by forty.

With only the thinnest of slippers the ballerina alights on the tips of her swollen toes, while her partner's poor feet land on the wooden stage with a high-impact thud only partially muffled by the orchestra. If, like opera, the discipline of ballet allowed its artists to voice their emotions, the air would be filled with cries of "Oh!", "Ooo!", and "Ow!"

Sitting as we do in the front row, I can make out the faint contours of elastic bandages around ankles, calves, and thighs. Below the waist dancers take a fearful beating during their weekly regimen of about forty hours of practice and rehearsals.

The battered ballerinas are best appreciated at a distance. Pity the guy who falls in love with one of them. As Oscar Wilde warned, he might end up with the only thing worse than not getting his heart's desire—and that is, getting it.

One of my male colleagues, a surgeon and a balletomane, fell in love with a prima ballerina. "It was the turn of her calf," he confided in me, "that gorgeous, balletic swell of her calf."

Obsessed with her career, she spurned his proposals for five years until repetitive injuries forced her to retire at thirty-seven. Then, reluctantly, she said yes to him—being a prima ballerina is a tough act to follow. For a while the surgeon was in seventh heaven. Her chiropractor was best man at their wedding. Her psychiatrist (eagerly) gave her away.

The surgeon retired to work round-the-clock treating his wife's chronic back sprain, her tenosynovitis of the long flexors of her great toes, her bunions, and her longing for acclaim. After two years of this, he began pining for the relative serenity of the operating room.

Three years after quitting the stage, she had gained twelve pounds and felt morbidly obese. Truth to tell, she looked more beautiful than she did as an anorectic dancer. Her husband tried to convince her of this fact one morning last year:

As she emerged through the shower curtains of their master bathroom, he clapped his hands vigorously and shouted, "Brava!" He then tossed a cellophane-wrapped bouquet at her aching feet. Smiling radiantly, she started her bow but slipped on the wet floor and bruised her left patella. He helped her back to bed where he joined her in what he describes as "a horizontal version of the *grand pas de deux* from *Swan Lake*."

She's been well ever since, proving that ballet is a physical and emotional disease that only love can cure.

28

The Bare Itch Project

THE HIT FILM *The Blair Witch Project* succeeds as a horror story not because one of the three young hikers disappears, but because the remaining two must suffer the agonies of hiking another day before they, too, vanish.

A forty-eight-hour hike in the woods is one of the few things yuppies can do to make them feel exactly like an eighty-year-old resident of a nursing home. I speak of low back pain, sore knees, swollen feet, constipation, itchy skin, insomnia, and disorientation.

Besides age, the main difference between the two groups is that if the yuppies survive the hike, they nurse their wounds at work in a cubicle before a PC monitor, whereas the old-timers, if they survive the night, nurse theirs in the day room before a TV screen.

It took civilization two thousand years to come out of the woods and what do millions of post-boomers do, including the three lost souls in the movie, but go back in! This is not a return to paradise but rather to parasites. Giardiasis follows a sip from that limpid brook.

Wearing backpacks made of lightweight material but filled with what appear to be lead ingots, the young hikers—armed with a 16mm camera, a Hi8 video camera, and a DAT sound recorder—set off on a misguided search for a mythical sylvan sorceress, aka the Blair Witch.

Now a witch is the only kind of being, male or female, who can survive in the woods: plenty of branches to fashion her broomsticks, lots of eyes of newt, toes of frog, and wool of bat to make her brew.

Flying above the trees, the elusive Blair Witch escapes Lyme disease, twisted ankles, snake bites, poison oak, bee stings, prying hikers, and bear claws.

She chews on St. John's Wort to enhance her cackle, nibbles on phytoestrogens to cool her hot flashes, applies herbal packs to prevent drying of the mole on her nose. She is, in short, one organic babe. If any hikers, such as the hapless trio in the film, should disturb her sylvan habitat, they become mulch.

Heather, the leader of the Blair Witch Project, grossly mismanages the search with an assist from one of the guys who throws away their map. It's refreshing to see in Heather a woman who achieves parity with man: shouting, cursing, scratching, and refusing to ask for directions. Hers is the first example of trail rage that's ever been filmed.

I concede there was no one around to ask directions of except perhaps the Blair Witch, but if Heather had brought along her PalmPilot, I bet she wouldn't have even asked Jeeves.

I'll never understand the allure of overnight hiking and camping. One of the easiest ways to poison a friendship is to share a tent, as the trio in the movie does. During their first night of sealing themselves in the weatherproof confines of the tent, one of the members noisily breaks wind. Now, a tent may protect its inhabitants from external forces of nature but actually serves to trap internal perturbations. Again, an instant nursing home experience.

The Blair Witch Project proves not only unhealthy for the hikers but for the movie audience as well. Heather leads the grungy trio in a long circle, painfully returning them and the audience to the creek bed where they had started.

Every miserable foot of this endless, circuitous slog is caught by their cameras in an out-of-focus, vertiginously jumpy film that had a third of the audience converting their half-eaten boxes of popcorn into barf bags.

On three separate occasions an audience member shouted, "Is there a doctor in the house?" There was no response from my sector since I was actually one of the nauseated patrons who called out for medical assistance. (Doctors who need doctors are the unluckiest people in the world.)

No one came to my rescue, although on my way out of the theater I recognized three of my colleagues. They were carrying their popcorn boxes at arm's length.

29

Voodoo Conversations
with a Zombie

I HADN'T BEEN TO NEW ORLEANS IN ALMOST FIFTY YEARS until last May when I delivered the commencement address to graduates of Louisiana State University's (LSU) Health Sciences Center.

Afterward, my ears bright pink from applause, I turned in my outsized cap and skimpy gown (I was, after all, cited in the program as a humorist) and headed for the French Quarter. I needed to unwind and to savor my biggest laugh from my oldest line: "If you drink, don't drive—if you smoke, don't bother wearing your seat belt."

The bar on Bourbon Street was named the Vee Zee, standing for, I soon learned, "Voodoo" and "Zombie." Inside and out, the Vee Zee was painted purple and gold—the official colors of Mardis Gras as well as the school colors of LSU. (And the way your eye looks two days after you remark to a Southern gentleman, "Surely, you can't still be chafing over the outcome of the Civil War!")

The semidarkened bar filled with air-conditioned smoke, was a refuge from the exhaust fumes and tropical heat of Bourbon Street. The ambience of the Vee Zee was studiously creepy. The jukebox played the mournful, slowed-down jazz of funeral marching bands. Under black lights, the lone cocktail waitress wore phosphorescent green makeup and a glowing white shroud that had seen better centuries.

The bartender was either an actual mummy or, on the advice of his lawyer after being rear-ended, was wearing the longest Ace bandage I'd ever seen.

Finding the last empty bar stool by the Braille method, I sat down and was handed a lagniappe of small objects, which, as my eyes adjusted to the gloom, turned out to be a pad of Post-its, a black ballpoint pen, and a shot glass full of pins. In lieu of salted peanuts or darts, this was Vee Zee's little offering of voodoo tools with which I could stick pins in a drawing of my worst enemy.

I'd heard of this punitive version of acupuncture but had never believed it had any more merit than, say, magnets for arthritis. Absently I sketched, then pierced, a rough self-portrait, complete with huge cap and tiny gown. (By coincidence I couldn't sleep that night due to pins-and-needles sensations in my arms and legs— undoubtedly, an allergic reaction to the shellfish in the excellent gumbo I'd had for dinner.)

"What'll it be?" asked the bartender in muffled tones.

"What's your house specialty?" I said.

"A double Vee & Zee."

"You don't want to go there," slurred a ghoulish young man seated next to me before a large tumbler of layered purple and gold liquid.

"Hell," I said, nodding to the bartender, "when in Rome . . . But make it a single."

With the first sip of my Vee & Zee I not only instantly relaxed, but also felt a sense of déjà vu so intense that for a moment I thought I was Yogi Berra.

"How long has the Vee Zee been in business?" I asked the bartender.

"Oh, about a hundred and twenty years."

The young man next to me tapped my elbow and asked, "Got a light?"

"No," I replied pompously. "I quit smoking the first day I started medical practice forty years ago."

"Wow, you've been a doctor twice as long as I've been alive," said the young man, accepting a light from the cocktail waitress.

Through the ambient smoke and black light, I could barely see that he was thin, had dark curly hair, and wore thick, horn-rimmed glasses. He looked vaguely familiar, possibly because I'd just given a speech to several hundred of his contemporaries.

"And if you keep smoking," I said, "I'm going to outlive you. . . . What do you do, may I ask?"

"Nothin'. I just finished my junior year in college. I'm majoring in journalism, but I'm considering a career as a zombie."

"One more of these," I said, raising my glass of Vee & Zee, "and you'll have passed your orals."

"Cheers," he said.

We each took a gulp, shuddered, and for a moment savored the sensation of being eternally dead.

"The only good thing about being a zombie," I observed, "is that you never have to worry about getting a health plan."

"Right now," he said, "I'm worried about getting a life. I once thought about being a doctor, but I was never interested in chemistry and math."

"Haven't you heard?" I said. "The practice of medicine is an art, not a science. You ought to think some more about being a doctor."

"Those dead bodies that medical students have to dissect are a total turn-off."

"Not at all. Our class learned more from our cadavers than from our professors. They were dug up from a pauper's grave outside of Columbia, Missouri, where I went to med school. They were twenty-three dead bodies teaching forty-six semicomatose students the rudiments of anatomy."

"The premedical students I know bore me to death."

"Let me quote from a speech I gave this morning," I said, clearing my throat. 'Some will tell you that the medical profession is under-rated, unhonored, underpaid, its members social drudges. I would rather tell you of a profession honorable above all others, one which, while calling for the highest powers of the mind, brings you into such warm personal contact with your fellow man that the heart and sympathies of the coldest nature must need be enlarged thereby.'"

"Powerful stuff," said the young man. "Did you make that up?"

"No. That was from the address of Sir William Osler, the greatest internist of all time, to the entering medical school class at McGill University in 1877."

The young man snuffed out his cigarette, pushed aside his Vee & Zee, and asked the bartender for a cup of black coffee.

"By the way," I said, leaving a ten-dollar bill on the teakwood bar and standing up, "where are you from?"

"St. Louis. I hitchhiked in this morning."

"Hey, I grew up in St. Louis," I said. "What's your name?"

For a few seconds, he didn't respond. As I pushed open the swinging doors to Bourbon Street, he replied, "Oscar London."

I turned fully around, and found myself standing outside a parking garage on Bourbon Street. I asked the middle-aged traffic cop on the corner, "What in hell happened to the Vee Zee bar?"

"Oh, that was torn down about ten years ago to make room for the garage."

"Hmm," I said, in my doctorly fashion.

30

An Indiscretion in the Footpath

DURING MY MORNING WALK on the service road that runs along the Mira Vista Golf Course in El Cerrito, California, I've grown bored with the usual flora (manicured greens) and fauna (manicured golfers). Perhaps I've caught spring fever, a disorder compounded of equal parts of hay fever, sleep deprivation, and romantic stirrings.

Yesterday morning as I walked, my somnambulation and sneezing were interrupted by a feathery commotion in the middle of the road. A pair of birds, which I later identified as either gilded flickers or McCown's longspurs, were in the midst of a mating dance.

The brightly plumed male was swaying his torso from side to side as he faced the bobbing head of the drab female. She was nodding her head, which, judging from her reluctance to start the mating process, is not an avian gesture of assent. I stood motionless, not fifteen feet away, as they continued their riveting dance.

I had awakened a bit late and was in a hurry to get my two-mile hike over with, but to barge through the mating ritual of two innocent birds was, I concluded, a crime against nature. I was not going to be personally responsible for endangering a species, whatever its name.

Last year during a late afternoon stroll, my wife and I stumbled across a teenage couple, uh, coupling in the grass atop Sutro Heights, a promontory in San Francisco overlooking the ocean. Discreetly we sidestepped these two birds of a different feather: the drab, sandy-crested male with a silver ring in his beak and the magenta-crowned, pierce-breasted female.

I conjectured at the time that the small metallic objects penetrating their flesh were a form of banding used by zoologists to monitor their migratory patterns. My wife suggested I try piercing my lips shut.

Getting back to the footpath near the golf course, I was growing increasingly annoyed with the two birds for taking too long to make up their minds. (I've become so removed from the natural rhythms and pace of nature that the time it takes for something to irritate me is rapidly approaching the speed of light.)

If I were a natural predator, the two birds endlessly dillydallying before me would be well on their way to being served boneless and herb-crusted as tonight's entrée. I know for a fact that whooping cranes wink just once at each other before making whoopee.

From time to time the male flicker (or longspur) would succeed in persuading the female to begin turning around, at which point he would shudder and walk a few paces away. She would then hop closer to him. What's with this guy? Was he possibly having erectile dysfunction? On this dying planet are we going to have to start sprinkling Viagra in the birdseed?

Even though all this posturing and conjecturing was taking place on a narrow, seldom-used roadway, every now and then a vehicle cautiously made an appearance. (The road services the elaborate homes of several millionaires who traditionally nest on the edges of golf courses.)

Just as the female had finally been coaxed into turning as much as forty degrees in clockwise rotation, a UPS truck slowly drove into view around the curve just behind us.

I stepped in front of the vehicle and waved the driver to stop. He glanced at his wristwatch and appeared very upset.

"I'm running late," he said. "What's the f_____g problem?"

"You've answered your own question," I replied, asking him to step out. I quickly proceeded to point out the delicate circumstances that prompted me to stay the swift completion of his appointed rounds.

In his UPS-issue short-sleeved shirt and khaki shorts, the thirty-ish driver looked very much the naturalist as he studied the two birds.

"What have I missed so far?" he asked.

"Nothing much," I replied, just as a FedEx truck rounded the corner. The UPS driver threw his body in front of the braking FedEx truck, narrowly averting a front-to-back mating of the two vehicles. I momentarily speculated that they could name the offspring of this union "Fed-Up," when the female bird suddenly turned a full half-circle.

This was the male bird's main chance.

Entranced, the two drivers and I witnessed the brief feathery consummation. I'd like to say that afterward the male bird picked up a cigarette butt from the roadside and took a deep drag, but, remember, this scene took place in smoke-free Northern California.

Like two movie stars caught *en flagrante delicto,* the two sated birds pointedly ignored us, declined to be interviewed, and flew off.

Giving the male bird's performance two thumbs up, the drivers climbed back into their respective vehicles and proceeded thoughtfully up the road. Momentarily cured of spring fever, I briskly resumed my walk.

31

The Seven Habits of Highly Obnoxious Patients

ALMOST ALL OF MY PATIENTS HAVE WINNING (as opposed to whining) personalities and are a pleasure to treat. A not so precious few are at the top of my list of people I'd rather not sit next to on a flight from Seattle to Sydney. If you can identify with any of these seven composite patients, you are driving your doctor to an early and welcome grave:

1. Sophia Logorrhea

She starts talking the moment I see her and doesn't pause for breath until I can manufacture some excuse (e.g., a fake fit of coughing) to get me out of the exam room. I never have to get pulmonary function tests on Sophia to assess her total lung capacity, her forced vital capacity, or her residual volume.

When I try to interrupt her, she interrupts my interruption. When I try to change the subject (her back pain, her sinuses, her indigestion), she offers the following unified theory:

"My postnasal drip got worse on your decongestants which made me so hyper all my back muscles tightened up so I took two ibuprofen like you said which lit up my heartburn like a bonfire and now I've got twenty Tums stacked up like poker chips in my esophagus and I feel awful all over and I have to baby-sit my granddaughter next weekend and let me show you her latest pictures, here, tell the truth, have you ever seen such a doll, and not to change the subject. . . ."

Overcome by a fit of coughing and self-pity, I lurch into the rest room where I rearrange the toiletries in the medicine cabinet for twenty minutes. This is barely enough time for Sophia to negotiate with my receptionist, Melodie, for her next appointment, at which time I plan to fly to Sydney. (As I fasten my seat belt and loosen my collar, an all too familiar voice next to me says, "Why, Dr. London, fancy meeting you here! As I was saying. . . ." I wake up screaming.)

2. Jack Nazdak

When I open the door to the exam room, Jack is using his cell phone and waves me away because it's a personal call. When I return ten minutes later, he's still on the phone and whispers to me, "It's my stockbroker, be with you in a jiff." Politely I protest, "That's okay, Jack, take your time. I have lots to do."

On my way out I can't help but admire Jack's new alligator loafers, which he wears over his bare feet. With what he paid for his designer-label, navy-blue blazer and his British worsted, pearl-gray slacks, one could buy a two-door Saturn. His HMO premiums set him back just fifty bucks a month. As much as I try, I can't expunge a mental image of his left alligator shoe biting his right ankle to the bone.

From my standard desktop phone in my consultation room, I end up having to phone Jack on his cell phone in Exam Room Two. He puts me on hold. Now his other ankle is bleeding.

When he finally talks to me on the phone, he says, "Morrie, you don't have to tell *me* my high-tech stocks are overvalued. . . ."

I respond, "This is not Morrie, this is your doctor speaking."

"Say, Doc, while I have you on the line, I get these terrific headaches."

"Which side of your head?"

"Right."

Suddenly I envision Jack's immediate future:

The OR, Alta Bates Hospital, Berkeley. In just over four hours Dr. Zigmund Klimt, my favorite neurosurgeon, excises a Nokia that's embedded itself into the right side of Jack's scalp. Deprived of his life support system, the patient promptly dies.

A common cause of death is anoxia, or lack of oxygen. This is my first case of anokia. Remember, you read it here first.

3. Janet Chondroitin

Anything I can do, her chiropractor, herbalist, and naturopath can do better. And then some. At least that's the message I seem to receive from Janet, age fifty-two, whenever I try to help her.

She's ingested so much shark cartilage and glucosamine for her aching knees that a horny fin has begun to grow from the center of her upper back. She wears her nascent, dorsal fin proudly and tells me, "At least it's not one of your damn 'placebo effects.'"

Spurning my traditional nostrums, she takes St. John's Wort for her depression, tofu for her hot flashes, and *Gingko biloba* for her short-term memory loss. When I ask her when she had her last hot flash, she says she can't remember and breaks down in tears.

Before they go to sleep, she and her husband tape magnets over their numerous, aching joints. They wake up in the morning sprawled on the floor on opposite sides of the bed. Refusing to admit they are magnetically or otherwise repelling each other, they've consulted a master of feng shui and their beloved chiropractor to realign their bed and their backs.

4. Seymour Jogalot

He's sixty-two, has an LDL cholesterol of 180, a blood pressure of 170/90, and insists he can bring these values down to normal with a better diet and more exercise. A ruthless competitor, he's won big-time in his global business ventures, doing it his way.

He wants to apply the same principles of self-reliance and ruthless hard labor to his health. He calls the local gym his "sweat shop." His BMI is already down to a svelte eighteen and he runs six hours a week. But his LDL and his blood pressure are still high.

I congratulate Seymour on his health habits, but also point out that he must take a "statin" and an ACE inhibitor to control his cholesterol and blood pressure.

"Those pills will ruin my sex life," he protests. "I'm sure I can bring my numbers down naturally." When I point out that if his optimal diet and maximum exercise program haven't lowered his cholesterol and blood pressure by now, they never will.

The pills I've recommended almost always work and have little or no sexual side effects. I implore him to at least try them.

"Doc, I don't want to be dependent on pills the rest of my life" are his last words before his first stroke.

He used to shake his head at my every suggestion. Now his head shakes all day long. I've always been struck by how horrible a bad stroke is compared to how easy it is to prevent.

After switching from being a jogger to using a walker, he still refuses to take medication. In the spirit of "never say die," I suggest just a pinch of Zestril for his blood pressure. With the middle finger of his weak right hand he's almost able to muster the strength to "flip me the bird," as his physical therapist describes what he's trying to do.

5. Mildred Ratched

At seventy-four, she doesn't look a day over fifty-five. Mildred dresses up for the doctor and treats him like a knight in shining armor (when actually it's my ten-year-old navy blue blazer that's gotten shiny). She's all charm, good humor, and flirtation. I think she's terrific and tell her so.

Then I learn from my office manager that she treats my staff like peons. Screams at them for not calling her pharmacy promptly, for trying to give her a late afternoon appointment instead of an early morning one, for putting her on hold, for not sending her a jury excuse by return mail (actually, my fault).

When I learn that this woman who dresses up for me dresses down my staff, I inform her that she'll have to distribute her courtesy evenly or find another office instantly.

She finds another office and as a parting shot gives my staff hell for taking so long to send a copy of my records to her new doctor.

The smart patient knows that the best way to get VIP treatment from me is to treat my staff like royalty.

6. Natalie Neversho

At forty-seven she has everything going for her: a new Lexus, beautiful hair, lovely nails, and excellent health insurance. Each November this rare, coveted PPO patient schedules an appointment for her yearly exam, then doesn't show.

By phone we reschedule Natalie, and a few days before her visit we call to remind her. She still doesn't show. And, unkindest cut of all, she doesn't even call to cancel. But when she wakes up with a tickle in her throat, she demands to be seen the same day.

When my receptionist asks her if she can come in the following day, she huffs, "I can't. I'm getting my nails done."

She's unclear on the concept that routine, well-patient visits tend to prevent emergency ones. Each November it's the same scene:

In deference to her PPO health plan, we have our biggest and best examining room all ready for her. My staff has laid out a snow-white paper gown and paper blanket, a paper-covered pillow, a clear plastic vaginal speculum brought to room temperature, an unpowdered pair of rubber gloves, a virgin tube of KY jelly, and a questionnaire. A current issue of *People* magazine awaits her on the end table. (Would we do all this for an HMO patient? Why do you ask?)

And then, a half-hour later, "Where's Natalie?"

It's like Charlie Chaplin's elaborate preparations for his own birthday party in *Gold Rush,* only to have no one show up.

In that film, Chaplin is so poor he boils one of his shoes and eats it for his entrée.

A few more patients like Natalie, who reserve a valuable hour on my appointment book and then don't show, and I'll be forced to dine on one of my old True Balance walking shoes. (For a truly balanced meal?) This filet of sole may be rubbery, but these days beggars can't be choosers. Chewers, yes; choosers, no.

I've tried boiling, I mean billing Natalie Neversho for missing her scheduled appointments. But she asks by return mail, "Why should I pay for an exam you never gave me?" Whenever I try to resign from her case, she shows up with chest pains on my doorstep.

Last week I told her that if she keeps this up, she'll be the death of me.

"Doctor London," she smiled, "please don't die before I do. Who will I get to renew my handicap parking sticker?"

"Don't worry, Natalie," I replied, "I wouldn't think of dying before you do. I wouldn't want to give you the satisfaction of not showing up at my funeral."

7. Barney Burnout

Barney gets only five hours of sleep, eats junk food, never takes the stairs, is always late, keeps people waiting, is overstressed and underpaid, drives too fast, and forgets his daily aspirin more often than not.

This seventh, highly obnoxious patient is me, aka Oscar London, and my refusal to improve my health habits has driven my illustrious, well-conditioned internist, Dr. Edward Waller, to early retirement. Which makes me envy him more than ever.

Now I must try to heal myself. But it's said that a doctor who treats himself has a fool for a patient and an idiot for a physician.

Duh, at least I can't sue myself.

32

A Drug-Drenched
Weekend in Vegas

SHE WAS, BY ANY CRITERION, A BEAUTIFUL BLONDE. Her black, low-cut, spaghetti-strap blouse and ultra-miniskirt left little of her physical beauty, especially her incandescent skin, to the imagination. In her early twenties, she was hanging on the arm of a fat, balding middle-aged man wearing an ill-fitting sport coat, baggy slacks, and a small diamond in his left earlobe.

She looked flushed with excitement as he led her to a small bench in the vast lobby of The Venetian hotel-casino. In her trembling right hand, she held a small white bag with a royal-blue logo on it that promised something very precious inside.

"Oh, I can't WAIT to put it on!" she cried.

She quickly sat down, crossed one perfect leg over the other, and pried off a new Ferragamo pump from her dainty foot.

"Ah," I thought, "her sugar daddy has bought her a diamond anklet."

Reaching into the bag, she whipped out a small box of Johnson & Johnson Band-Aids and dexterously taped one over an angry-looking blister on her right heel. Slipping her shoe back on, she stood up and sighed with relief.

"Thanks, Pop," she said, kissing her father on his stubble-bearded cheek. I noticed that the elegant, blue calligraphy on the opened white bag spelled "Walgreens."

Her Dad noticed me staring at her and scowled. Then smiled. "Oscar, you old goat, are you here for the conference too?"

Through the stubble, I suddenly recognized the face of a San Francisco internist I'd known vaguely for years.

"Oscar, I'd like you to meet my daughter, Jessica. In a few years she'll give you a run for the money as the 'World's Best Doctor.'"

I could feel my face flush as I shook their extended hands.

So much for my vaunted diagnostic skills. I'd mistaken a medical student for a bimbo.

This was not the last time Las Vegas would distort my sense of reality.

Last weekend my wife and I, along with 950 other doctors and spouses, were in Vegas as the guests of a multibillion-dollar drug cartel. Their reps were trying to persuade us to prescribe their brand name of a cholesterol-lowering drug, which actually is no better or worse than five other "statins" on the market.

We were put up in an opulent suite at The Venetian, the Strip's newest hypertrophied hotel-casino. When its building program is completed, The Venetian will be the biggest hotel in the world, housing over seven thousand guests. An odor-free replica of the Grand Canal—complete with water, gondolas, singing gondoliers, and wide-eyed American tourists—runs through the shopping mall on the second, I repeat, second floor. (You wouldn't want the Grand Canal to bisect the first-floor casino, would you? High-stakes losers might toss themselves in like so many discarded nickels.)

To keep our mood elevated and receptive, our hosts, the drug reps, did everything they could to discourage us from gambling, that is, from losing. They drove us like pampered mules to continental breakfasts in the morning, to guided tours of Hoover Dam in the afternoon, and at night to four-star restaurants and glitzy shows.

Despite the reps' heroic efforts they were not able to conceal the 120,000-square-foot casino on the ground floor of the Venetian. In this vaulted, Vatican-sized enclosure, there is seating room at the slot machines and blackjack tables for 6,200 buttocks. That comes to slightly more than 200 square feet per buttocks, which should provide each guest with ample wiggle room no matter how much junk food they consume at the casino buffets.

Astonished, we doctors observed pathology everywhere we looked. Rarely does one get to see the rear ends of so many of life's losers in one place. To the relief of the reps, we were appalled at what we could dimly perceive through the suffocating pall of cigarette smoke. The slotsuckers held large cups that they used to beseech alms from Mammon, the one-armed god before whom they sat praying for hours, sometimes days. Like a mendicant begging for coins in the streets of Calcutta, the slotsucker ended each day with an empty cup.

Sick City Syndrome

Move over, Calcutta—make room for Vegas. Both cities suffer in their own way from overcrowding, poverty, air pollution, and ghastly nutrition. Both Calcuttans and Las Vegans worship their dead: ancestors in Calcutta, Elvis Presley in Vegas. In India, a vegan eats greens; in Nevada, a Vegan eats beef. In India, history is measured in millennia; in Vegas, in months. Less than a year ago you'd have had no trouble finding a three-dollar blackjack table in Vegas. Nowadays the minimum bet all over town starts at ten bucks, which means you can hemorrhage ten thousand dollars in four hours and not know it until you stand up and pass out.

Nervously we doctors compared notes: Not even neurosurgeons, we agreed, can afford to gamble at these stakes.

Only at the Luxor, an ancient casino-hotel that opened in early 1996, did I find a prehistoric relic—a three-dollar blackjack table. With such a small minimum bet, I figured that even I could afford to lose a few bucks. At least thirty patrons stood waiting for a seat to become vacant at the crowded table. I asked one of them how long he'd been waiting and he said, "Only four months."

"Why does it take so long?" I asked.

"The only way you get a seat at a three-dollar table is when one of the players dies of natural causes."

This contrasts with the sudden death you can witness at a five-hundred-dollar table at the Bellagio. A handsome, well-groomed man in his fifties, wearing a four-thousand-dollar Armani blazer, seated in casual elegance at a five-hundred-dollar table, drops eighty thousand in forty-five minutes, at which point he clutches his chest and slumps to the floor.

Pretending to escort a drunk out of the casino, two pit bosses drag the body in a standing position to the Bellagio's conservatory garden. They hustle the loser into the ground faster than a blackjack dealer burying the first card at the bottom of a new deck.

In a town famous for quickie marriages and divorces, the quickie burial has become the latest attraction.

Behold the Strip: Like smooth white casts covering hideously damaged tissue, the glitzy exteriors of high-rise pleasure palaces encase the gangrenous disease of gambling. Succumbing to this sickness, our host, the drug cartel, bet a million dollars that we doctors, out of gratitude for this free weekend in Vegas, would prescribe their cholesterol-lowering drug to hundreds of our coronary-prone patients for the rest of their lives. If just a third of us knuckled under to their blandishments, their million-dollar bet would garner a payoff of at least fifty-to-one. After they softened our brains with nonstop entertainment, booze, and food, the cartel's bet was a lot safer than that of any other game in town.

The reason Las Vegas can afford to put up hotel-casinos costing $1.5 billion (Venetian) and $1.6 billion (Bellagio) is the greed and obsession of the amateur gambler. The amateur never quits when he's ahead. His greed keeps him playing through several winning streaks until the immutable odds in favor of the house finally do him in.

Reincarnations of Venice, Caesar's Rome, Manhattan, and Paris rise phoenixlike from the cigarette ashes of addicted gamblers on the Strip. Obscene profits from the blackjack tables alone could account for the amazing Bellagio Gallery of Fine Art. This guilt offering to the fleeced public features works, not replicas, of Van Gogh, Picasso,

Rembrandt, Degas, Cezanne, Manet, and Matisse, to name a few unlikely inhabitants of a hotel on the Strip.

Degas in Vegas—a mind-boggling concept.

Only one of Van Gogh's paintings, *The Red Vineyard*, sold in his lifetime. The buyer paid the equivalent of $25. It recently cost $60 million to let Van Gogh's *Peasant Woman* hang out at the Bellagio. Vincent finally got lucky in Vegas.

Conscious of the vulnerability of our derrieres, my wife and I refused to sit at the slots or at the blackjack tables. And so, with the exception of having sold our souls to a drug cartel, we left Vegas big winners.

33

Class of '48

Old Doctors Never Die...

SOME YEARS AGO I attended my fiftieth high school reunion, otherwise known as a near-death experience. With 63 of us already dead, we were 240 survivors of University City High School, in the lovely suburbs of St. Louis, Class of '48, the year apartheid was made legal in South Africa.

Sixty-three of us dead. This high school massacre was not the impulsive act of a teenage boy with an automatic weapon but rather the slow, steady work of an old man with a scythe.

My fellow alums, half of them Jewish, half WASPS, living in harmony then, surviving in harmony now: Sagging cheerleaders! Hemiplegic track stars! Bypassed heartthrobs! Speech-impaired valedictorians! Bald Romeos! Wrinkled Juliets! And then, yours truly, happier and more energetic than the nerd I was at eighteen, a silver fox among the molting pelts. How did I do it?

The gene pool of my mother, who recently died after ninety-four vigorous years. Any questions?

Two drop-dead beauties appeared among the female alums—at our age, "drop-dead" is a freighted adjective. To my practiced eye these formerly plain teenagers were transformed in recent years by their plastic surgeons. Facial skin smooth as porcelain dolls by Jumeau. Dressed to their veneered teeth in haute couture. Great figures! (Tummy tucked? Lipo-sucked? Tushes hiked? As a gracefully aging Midwestern gentleman, I thought it polite not to ask.)

The huge diamonds on their left ring fingers called attention to their slightly prominent knuckles and their very prominent husbands. As teenagers these two gorgeous sexagenarians pursued our football team's quarterback in vain.

At the fiftieth reunion the former quarterback, standing tall beside his walker, gamely made a pass at his two former groupies by winking at them. They didn't give him the time of day. Clutching his chest for a moment, the old quarterback leaned forward and confided in me, "Oscar, after sixty-five, we all enter sudden-death overtime."

Many of us hadn't seen each other in fifty years. In '48 our careers and families were our fondest dreams; in '98 they are our history, embellished in our minibiographies for the *Fiftieth Anniversary Directory of Classmates.*

At thirty-three, one of us had climbed Everest in the first American ascent. I'm tempted to say he peaked too soon, but Tom Hornbein went on to become the head of the anesthesiology department for sixteen years at the University of Washington. He recently spent several weeks at 18,000 feet doing high altitude research. Last week I raced my six-year-old granddaughter, Haley, up the back steps of my house and won. She cried, but she has *her* whole life ahead of her.

The final banquet was held in a glassed-in ballroom on the luxurious grounds of the fin de siècle Shaw's Garden in South St. Louis. As former student body president, I was asked to say a few words. In looking through the classroom directory, I noticed that the master of ceremonies, Bill Shoss, boasted that he was the sales director thirty years ago of the first refrigerator magnets.

I told my classmates that I was reminded of one of my patients, a petite sixty-year-old woman who, lacking the sweetness of a Midwestern upbringing, has roundly criticized my drug therapy for her chronic back pain. Through the years everything I tried, from Naprosyn to Ultram, only added side effects to her back pain.

She finally hit on the latest alternative fad for treatment of chronic pain, namely old-fashioned magnets. Each morning her husband, before he left for work, dutifully taped a powerful, $300 magnet to the spot where her back hurt most—right between her shoulder blades. The patient loved to tell me how much relief her magnet was giving her compared to my toxic nostrums.

One morning as she scurried about her kitchen in a flimsy bathrobe, her magnet securely taped in place, she passed within a foot of her refrigerator and SWACK!—she was slammed back into the metal door. Until her husband returned eight hours later, she was stuck fast. She took her place among her other refrigerator magnets including one that bore a reminder that she take her 3:00 P.M. dose of St. John's Wort.

A few minutes after my classmates kindly applauded my magnet story, one of the female alums sat down next to me and demurely raised the hem of her skirt to reveal five circular one-inch diameter magnets taped around her somewhat knobby right knee. She swore by her little magnets.

I could only despair that alternative medicine had moved into the nation's heartland from the West Coast—just as I had, into Missouri from California, to gaze briefly at my teenage years through very moist eyes.

At midnight, under a sudden spotlight, a pastel-garbed big band materialized on the stage at the far end of the room. Soon slow dance music from the forties caressed the air. As the overhead lights dimmed, we grabbed our partners.

Transformed by the subdued, peachy-pink light and the nostalgic emanations from clarinets, saxes, and trombones, we suddenly looked for all the world like a twentieth high school reunion not a fiftieth. As long as we could keep the band playing and the lights low, we were young again. After fifty years this old doctor discovered that nostalgia was the elixir of youth. And the band played on.

Long live the Class of '48!

34

The Fowl Manners of
the Canada Goose

LIKE SO MANY OUT-OF-TOWNERS, Canada geese love to summer in the San Francisco Bay Area where the lawns are lush, green, and delicious. These handsome tan, white, and black birds are admirable in all ways but one: The bowels of the Canada geese are loose, with a "throughput" (as the ornithologists say) of ninety minutes from grass to guano.

This rapid transit time is characteristic of the species—I remember George C. Scott, in the movie *Patton*, exhorting his troops to "go through the German lines like crap through a goose!"

This metaphor may have been instrumental in winning World War II, but it's threatening to destroy the golf courses, parks, lawns, lakes, and swimming pools of suburban America. The bacterial content of a Canada goose dropping is probably not harmful to humans, but this is a matter of some controversy. Until further clarification of its effects, Bay Area suburbanites are encouraged to drink, bathe in, and swim in Evian water.

Apart from their unfortunate bowel habits, the Canada geese are lovely creatures. "They've got family values out the wazoo," according to one of their more birdbrained human admirers.

First of all, Canada geese are monogamous. They mate for life—

no messy divorces, fly-by-night feather ruffling, or honking at chicks preening themselves on street corners.

Canada geese make excellent parents, teaching their offspring complicated migratory routes, instructing them on how to communicate with ten different honks, and insisting their goslings follow them in single file.

They fly in a distinctive "V" pattern, probably to avoid getting mud in their eye.

According to a recent article in the *San Francisco Examiner,* the droppings of countless thousands of Canada geese in the Bay Area are destroying the lawns and shoes of the finest families. Affluent, well-shod homeowners are up in arms, resorting to drastic measures to encourage the once-loved Canada goose to go home and never come back.

One method is to hire dogs from a company called "Goose Busters." (I am not making this up.) The dogs are trained to charge the geese and send them scurrying to a neighbor's lawn, but not before presumably scaring more poop out of them.

Another antigoose technique is to addle their eggs, which are being laid in wild profusion around local ponds and lakes. Addling consists in smothering the eggs in oil and requires a government permit. These addlepated advocates of addling have obviously forgotten that the oily bird gets the worm. (But I'll forgive their lapse, if you'll forgive my pun.)

To the horror of the Humane Society some communities have taken to exterminating their geese with permission from the government. If this practice becomes widespread, it might succeed in endangering the species and thereby reinstating the Canada goose as an object of affection. Many Americans would rather see the Canada goose on a postage stamp than on their front lawn.

These same citizens slap their grandfathers in nursing homes as soon as the geezers, like the geese, lose control of their bowels. As the baby boomers age, we'll quickly run out of nursing-home space. With further shrinking of the medical dollar, I fear we'll be warehousing our incontinent elderly in structures built on the chicken-ranch model.

Are you absolutely sure you want to continue taking your cholesterol-lowering pill?

Public bird sanctuaries in the Bay Area are not helping the avian situation by feeding day-old gourmet bagels to the pullulating geese. Armed with garlic breath, the ceaselessly honking Canada goose has repelled competing species such as the easily offended trumpeter swan.

May I modestly propose that the day-old bagels be sprayed with paregoric before being fed to the geese? This coating will create lawn-sparing constipation and gas. As they achieve a critical mass of gas, the geese will gently levitate on the next southerly and waft gently back to Canada.

35

Take Two Adenine and Call Me in the Morning: Genomic Medicine Fifteen Years from Now

From the Online Diary of Dr. Oscar London

June 27, 2015, 3:12 P.M.

Ever since scientists announced they had completed the map of the human genome in the year 2001, my office phones have been ringing off the hook. Everybody wants a copy of their customized "Instruction Book of Life" ASAP so they can correct some of their imperfections before it's too late. Here are segments of recent e-mail correspondence with my genomically uptight patients:

7/2/2015
dear dr. london—

thanks for e-mailing me a copy of my genome for which I gave a blood sample to your lab in april. sorry it took you three weeks on your mac just to send me the data. i wish you'd bill me. (just kidding) i spent a month printing my genome off your e-mail with my epson. it was like watching my whole life pass before me!

i then crated it and shipped it by amtrak for interpretation to the joint genome institute in walnut creek, california.

imagine my shock when i was informed today that my own personal genome is that of a fourteen-year-old chimpanzee! what is more, the institute has officially listed me as a chimpanzee with the human genome project!! my son the lawyer is climbing the walls since he heard about this. please advise. sincerely, max esterhazy

dear mr. esterhazy—

it's those damn hmos again. they're too cheap to print out all 3.1 billion subunits of your dna. at best, they identify about 80 percent of a patient's complete genome—and, as you know, we human beings share 98 percent of our genetic material with the chimpanzee.

if being certified a chimpanzee continues to trouble you, you can be reclassified as a homo sapiens by appearing any thursday before 9:00 A.M. at the primate house of the san francisco zoo. ask mr. gibbon for the necessary test forms (warning: half of adult californians have the reading skills of a marmoset).

mr. esterhazy, if i were you, i'd just forget about the whole thing. try to forgive a tiny 2 percent lab error. relax, eat a banana, and groom your mate. (just kidding)

this grievous genomic error inflicted on you is yet another example of how the hmos are making monkeys of us all. o.london, m.d.

dr. london—

f.y.i., a chimpanzee is an ape, not a monkey. m. esterhazy.

dear mr. esterhazy—

whatever. i suppose it takes one to know one. o. london, m.d.

✸ ✷ ✦

7/5/2015
Dear Doc—

Since the language of the human genome consists of varying combinations of the letters T, A, C, and G (standing for the four proteins of DNA), I thought you might enjoy the very first genomic joke.

A buff Y chromosome walks into a saloon and sees a ravishing X chromosome seated at the bar. "AT/AT/CG very often?" asks the Y chromosome, ordering a martini. "GC/TA, often enough," she replies. "Well, TA/CG, your AT, or mine?" he says, placing his hand on her knee. She plucks a toothpick with two speared olives from his drink, munches down the olives, and snaps the toothpick in two. "XY, are you sure, TA/CG you're man enough for XX?" she asks, looking down at his fly.

"AT/CG/CG/XY, outta here!" he says, running for the door. ("G")

Your patient, Nora Winston

✹ ★ ★

6 July 2015
My Dear Dr. Oscar London,

As you know, 95 percent of the human genome is composed of chemical bonds having no apparent purpose. Geneticists call them "junk DNA." We here at green/genes.com call them "junk bonds."

For as little as $5,000, you, Dr. Oscar London, CAN OWN THE EXCLUSIVE PATENT ON TWENTY-FIVE JUNK BONDS! Yes, Dr. Oscar London, you stand to realize an 800 percent return of investment in the first thirty days or your stamped, self-addressed envelope will be returned to you, no questions asked.

If, as futurists predict, these seemingly inert links will someday prove of vast importance to our health and longevity, your first-year royalties, Dr. Oscar London, will approximate the gross national product of Ecuador!

To each of the first one billion lucky investors who purchase twenty-five of our junk bonds, Dr. Oscar London, we will send a handsome coffee mug inscribed with the logo of our cloning division: "There's One Born Every Minute."

So hurry, Dr. Oscar London. Your telomeres are shortening as you read this!

Sincerely yours,
Erskine Spam, Esq., CEO, green/genes.com

36

Are You Too Old for Romantic Love?

ROMANTIC LOVE is one of the worst things that can happen to a teenager and one of the best to an old-timer. For starters look what romantic love did to Romeo and Juliet. If they had met in their seventies instead of their early teens, their feuding parents would have been long dead and they could have tottered unchallenged down the aisle.

(*West Side Story* would have taken place in a nursing home and the hero's loud, poignant cry of "Maria!" would have fallen on deaf ears due to battery failure in her hearing aid.)

I believe that, to propagate our species, romantic love is hardwired into all of us at age thirteen. In our society, as opposed, say, to early nineteenth-century Tahiti, young romantic love not infrequently leads to unwanted pregnancy, even more unwanted disease, premature marriage, ill-timed parenthood, arrested education, and worst of all, appearances on the *Jerry Springer Show.*

On the other hand, old romantic love can cure depression as well as improve virtually all other diseases known to man or woman.

Last month I met Emily, whose daughter insisted that she see me for some balm for her grief.

Emily was seventy-five and Leonard, eighty-two, when they met at an art museum. They spent two and a half blissful years together before he died last month of agonizingly painful bone cancer, the first symptoms of which had begun a few months before they met.

His oncologist had given Leonard half of the standard six months to live. Emily and Leonard's romantic love initially allowed him to cut his narcotic dose by two-thirds and, ultimately, to live ten times longer than predicted.

She had kept much of her young beauty, featuring a radiant smile, large amethyst eyes, "high colour," as the British say, in her complexion, and a shapely figure. Her fine blonde hair had turned a gleaming silver.

From a photograph she showed me, he looked like Henry Fonda in *On Golden Pond.*

Weeping softly through half a box of Kleenex, she told me that, toward the end, Leonard still refused heavy narcotics, explaining that "he wanted to be alert enough to see me, kiss me, and talk to me."

Each night he would say, "I hate to go to sleep because I won't be able to see you 'til morning." And the day before he died, he said, "If I were given the choice of being pain-free for ten years but without you or being able to live one extra day in this much pain but with you, I'd gladly choose that extra day with my darling."

At that I appropriated one of my own Kleenex.

Talking to me of their love seemed to help her at once. At the end of the hour I prescribed a mild stimulant by day and a sleeping pill at night. She called me a week later to thank me for easing the most acute phase of her pain.

Leona, age sixty-six, called herself "a real American—one-third Native American, one-third African-American, and one-third honky." With a touch of makeup, she looked forty-six and had enough symptoms to keep eight doctors busy. And that's exactly what her symptoms did: kept four doctors scratching their heads in Berkeley and another four agitating their scalps across the bay in San Francisco.

After twelve years of trying to help Leona, I had scratched myself almost bald. As her primary care doctor I had referred her to three specialists in Berkeley, hoping to help her and to preserve what little sanity and hair I had left. The four doctors in San Francisco I would learn about later.

Repeated efforts to extricate myself from her care met with tearful pleadings from Leona and her very extended family to keep her in my practice. She made an appointment at least once a month and whether her symptom du jour was headache, abdominal pain, joint stiffness, or tiredness, I could never help her.

I tried to persuade her that she had been clinically depressed ever since her long-suffering daughter had evicted her from the family home and banished her to a nice apartment in Oakland. She wouldn't hear of it—"Me depressed? Are you crazy?"

Every time a new antidepressant came on the market, I prescribed it for her "to help your aches and pains." I hoped she'd take it for a few weeks and finally get some relief. But she always caught on within forty-eight hours. "You can't fool old Leona, Doctor—I can smell an SSRI a mile away!"

She was unwilling to take antidepressants but was liberal about every other medication in the U.S. pharmacopoeia. At one point she was taking eighteen of my prescription drugs with nary a side effect, nor a desired effect.

Leona was the most accomplished professional patient I'd ever known. The four doctors she saw in San Francisco were a secret she kept from me for ten years. Thanks to three separate medical policies she had inherited from as many deceased husbands, she was able to sign on with another primary care doctor in San Francisco, who, out of self-preservation, also found it necessary to refer her to three specialists—a neurologist, a rheumatologist, and a gastroenterologist, duplicating my three Berkeley referrals.

Leona managed to keep her San Francisco medical life a secret from me until I received a muffled phone call from one of her fourteen children, swearing me to secrecy. He said his mother would kill him if she found out:

"Momma's got a whole set of doctors in San Francisco you don't know about, Dr. London—and a chiropractor in San Jose! And I'm getting tired of carrying her all over Berkeley and San Francisco AND San Jose!"

Before I could figure out a way to confront Leona with this revelation, she disappeared from my practice.

Two months later she showed up in my waiting room, twenty pounds lighter and looking age thirty-six. She had a dazzling white-toothed smile, which I had never seen before. "Doctor London, I'm off all medications and I feel like a million dollars," she beamed.

As proof that love is color blind, she introduced me to "Jack," her Irish-American, blushing beau, a carpenter who had just turned fifty and didn't look a day over seventy-five. Wearing a deer hunter's cap, with his nicotine-stained fingers and more than a faint trace of Jack Daniels on his breath, he was a poster boy for the Bureau of Alcohol, Tobacco, and Firearms.

From isolated family reports over the next year, I learned that Leona remained in complete remission. She and Jack behaved like newlyweds. And Leona completely cured Jack of his addictions. Because they couldn't keep their hands off each other, Jack was no longer able to smoke, drink, or hunt.

A year later Jack fell off the wagon, then off a roof, and died. Leona was back on my doorstep with a broken heart and eighteen empty pill bottles. Between sobs she repeated what her grandmother had often told her, "Mens is no good."

After offering my sincere condolences, I resigned from her care and she quickly found another internist in Oakland.

She would have been much better off finding another lover in Berkeley.

★ ✶ ★

Sylvia, seventy-seven, was well-to-do and slender. Over the years she invested a small fortune in cosmetic surgery, with impressive gains in her face value. She liked to quote the famous adage "You can't be rich enough or thin enough" to which she added in her husky voice, "or young enough."

She had been happily married for thirty-two years until 1970 when her husband, an exceedingly prosperous businessman, died in his fifties of a stroke. The widowed Sylvia was a far different person from the married Sylvia.

In a word, she was mean. Whenever I asked her, "How are you?" she answered, "Lousy—and the pills you gave me last time almost killed me!"

When I finally suggested she find another doctor, she refused, probably sensing that I was able to take patient abuse better than anyone else she might choose.

Her diagnoses were the internist's terrible trinity: chronic fatigue syndrome, fibromyalgia, and chronic pain syndrome. I exhausted every neurologist, rheumatologist, and pain specialist in town.

I often thought that all of us Sylvia—failed physicians should form a support group. But then who wants to see a bunch of grown men cry? Better we should sob in the privacy of our consultation room with the door closed.

Sylvia insisted on taking high doses of hydrocodone, a narcotic, for relief of her misery. I couldn't get her off of it and deeply regretted ever getting her on it. According to Rosa, her martyred live-in attendant, she swallowed her tenth dose of hydrocodone each night with four ounces of Tanqueray gin over ice.

She was living proof that the human organism can survive fifty years of a three-pack-a-day cigarette habit. Sylvia had marvelous genes—both parents lived to be over a hundred: "They were never sick a day in their life until the day they died. Mom lived an hour longer than Dad."

Despite my best efforts Sylvia remained a very unmerry widow. She never recovered from her husband's death. Until she and an eighty-two-year-old retired pediatrician began their three-year affair.

His young patients (including, in their childhood, Sylvia's three boys) called him "Doctor Manny" during his forty-year practice. Now, widowed for ten years, he'd been an old family friend.

One night Manny graciously accompanied Sylvia, as he had for years, to Rosh Hashanah services at an Oakland temple. Fidgety by nature, he accidentally, so the story goes, touched Sylvia's knee an hour into the service. Before he could apologize and withdraw his hand, Sylvia grabbed it and held on for dear life.

Sylvia dropped out of my practice. For three years the only contact I had with her was a phone call to me (I didn't recognize her cheerful voice at first) asking me to renew her estrogen prescription before she and Manny left for a cruise to Europe on the *QEII*.

When Sylvia returned, broken, to me after Manny's sudden death in Venice, she tearfully reminisced about his courtliness, his attentiveness, and his amorousness. "Unlike you," she told me, "Manny never once complained about my smoking. He sent me flowers every week and got me off of gin and onto champagne."

For an eighty-two-year-old guy in the pre-Viagra era, Manny, by Sylvia's account, was the cat's meow. At least five times a week.

Manny was more powerful than any drug in the *Physicians' Desk Reference*. For Sylvia his only side effect was euphoria. After Manny died, Sylvia went back on hydrocodone to recapture at least a little euphoria. Sylvia died ten years later, at the age of eighty-six. A month before her demise, Sylvia confided in me, "I was much happier parting my lips for one of Manny's kisses than for one of your pills."

37

In the Theatre of Medicine, Are You a Star or an Extra?

TO SURVIVE A FRIDAY AFTERNOON IN MY OFFICE, it helps me to recall Shakespeare's view that "all the world's a stage, and all the men and women, merely players. . . ."

As a solo practitioner in the age of HMOs, I sometimes feel like the head of a small, struggling theatrical company on the verge of closing in Berkeley. I, of course, play the leading role of Doctor. My repertory company is rounded out by a comedienne (my secretary) and a tragedienne (my bookkeeper).

The patients flesh out our little troupe, furiously changing costumes, suddenly laughing, crying, and sighing as they briefly recite their monologues before Doctor interrupts with one of his own.

As it is on the stage, makeup is crucial. If one of my ingénues is interested in getting a doctor's note from me stating that she's too ill to work, she carefully applies a light ivory foundation over her forehead and cheeks, brushes purple shadow under her eyes, and spends a great deal of time on her hair, teasing it into a fright wig. As for her costume, she dresses not to kill but rather to die. (Black is the favorite color here.)

This bit of stagecraft, combined with her genuine snuffles and mild cough, is enough to award her something more valuable than a Tony:

a doctor's hand-illuminated excuse from work, suitable for framing (her boss).

Once a patient went to the extreme of wearing a bathrobe to my office! For this she received what we call in my office an "Oscar": a doctor's excuse plus a prescription for Prozac.

The theater of medicine is not without its props. With frequent wincing, a sixty-year-old patient with mild osteoarthritis of his knees shuffles into my office leaning on a four-footed Canadian cane. For months he's been trying to persuade me to write out a doctor's most coveted prescription: certification for a handicap parking sticker. I sternly rebuff his pleas and ask him to try Celebrex.

The next prop he uses, ineptly, is a walker. (I had caught sight of him the previous Saturday afternoon walking jauntily up to the seventh green of the golf course across the street from our house.) I remind the patient that unless I'm totally convinced he's disabled, it would be easier for him to pull out my incisors than to get a handicap sticker out of me.

At his next visit his wife, in a supporting role, propels him to the exam room in a wheelchair. At last here's my chance to play Big Daddy in *Cat on a Hot Tin Roof*:

"Sir," I declare, "I detect a strong odor of mendacity in this room. Two weeks ago I happened to see you walking unassisted on a golf course."

"Yeah," he protests, "but now I can't play more than three holes, and I gotta use a golf cart."

I promptly write out a prescription for a handicap sticker for his golf cart.

[CURTAIN]

In the theater of the absurd, which is my office on a Friday afternoon, my standard opening lines are "Good to see you! You look wonderful!" (Pasty face, oversized black dress, and misshapen hair notwithstanding.)

Old trouper that I am, I try to recite "You look wonderful!" to each patient as if for the first time. Last Friday I rehearsed these lines to myself in front of the mirror in my office rest room—a totally unconvincing performance.

[CURTAIN]

As a patient, you are the playwright and the star in your own real life drama. If you insist, portray yourself as the hero and, if appropriate, your supervisor or your spouse as the villain. This is your chance to strut and fret your quarter-hour upon the stage. If you have stage fright, take a Xanax.

Our assuming the roles of modest patient and omnipotent doctor inhibits your ability to get well. In the short time your doctor allots for your monologue, pull out all stops, hold nothing back. No matter how shocking you may think your material is, your doctor has heard it all before and, in my case, at least three times.

And don't hesitate to interrupt your doctor's interruption. "Please let me finish" is a line you should rehearse before every doctor's visit.

In the final appraisal of your medical performance, it's often not so much what you say that leads to a successful catharsis (in its psychological, gastrointestinal, or theatrical sense). Rather it's the little pieces of business you subconsciously use while you're emoting.

I'm referring to the sudden downward glance of the young man reluctant at first to talk about his fear of having herpes. Or the eyelid twitch when I ask a young woman who's been married six months how things are going at home and she says, "Fine."

I speak of the fleeting movement of the tips of a patient's thumb and index finger to his or her nostrils as a dead giveaway that the patient associates the subject under discussion with noxious emanations from the nether regions of the body. (I am modestly dubbing this revealing piece of business, London's Sign. It does not refer to the odor of mendacity.)

In the theater a writer who's called in to improve a script is known as a "doctor." I like to think that without a doctor you will suffer the fate of Mercutio and Tybalt in *Romeo and Juliet*, who die young on stage well before the final curtain. If Romeo hadn't killed Tybalt, he and Juliet would have ended up as an old married couple shouting at each other to put out the cat. "Out, damned cat!"

A Shakespearean nightmare I suffer recurrently involves my having a day in the office that resembles *Hamlet*. It's a Friday afternoon, the worst time in a doctor's week, and day's end finds six corpses strewn on the floor, including mine. A combination of poisons and swordplay has done us in. A young depressed woman floats Ophelialike through my office and tries to drown herself in the bathroom sink.

I wake up screaming and drive to work. It is indeed Friday, but by late afternoon all of us are still alive! My patients have taken penicillin and Prozac instead of poison. And, rather than dying by the sword, three are saved by my scalpel.

And I'm not even a surgeon!

[BLACKOUT]

★ ✱ ★